DATE DUE

Garbage and Recycling

Other Books of Related Interest:

At Issue Series

The Energy Crisis

The Local Food Movement

Nuclear and Toxic Waste

Current Controversies Series

Conserving the Environment

The Green Movement

Nuclear Energy

Oil

Vegetarianism

Global Viewpoints Series

Climate Change

Population Growth

Introducing Issues with Opposing Viewpoints Series

Globalization

Health Care

Nuclear Power

Organic Food and Farming

Opposing Viewpoints Series

China

Consumerism

Energy Alternatives

Global Warming

Globalization

Water

GLOBALVIEWPOINTS

Garbage and Recycling

Candice Mancini, Book Editor

GREENHAVEN PRESS
A part of Gale, Cengage Learning

GALE
CENGAGE Learning

Detroit • New York • San Francisco • New Haven, Conn • Waterville, Maine • London

GALE
CENGAGE Learning™

Christine Nasso, *Publisher*
Elizabeth Des Chenes, *Managing Editor*

© 2011 Greenhaven Press, a part of Gale, Cengage Learning

Gale and Greenhaven Press are registered trademarks used herein under license.

For more information, contact:
Greenhaven Press
27500 Drake Rd.
Farmington Hills, MI 48331-3535
Or you can visit our Internet site at gale.cengage.com

For product information and technology assistance, contact us at

Gale Customer Support, 1-800-877-4253
For permission to use material from this text or product, submit all requests online at www.cengage.com/permissions

Further permissions questions can be emailed to permissionrequest@cengage.com

Articles in Greenhaven Press anthologies are often edited for length to meet page requirements. In addition, original titles of these works are changed to clearly present the main thesis and to explicitly indicate the author's opinion. Every effort is made to ensure that Greenhaven Press accurately reflects the original intent of the authors. Every effort has been made to trace the owners of copyrighted material.

Cover image copyright © Ashley Cooper/Corbis.

LIBRARY OF CONGRESS CATALOGING-IN-PUBLICATION DATA

Garbage and recycling / Candice Mancini, book editor.
    p. cm. -- (Global viewpoints)
    Includes bibliographical references and index.
    ISBN 978-0-7377-5081-2 (hardcover) -- ISBN 978-0-7377-5082-9 (pbk.)
    1. Refuse and refuse disposal. 2. Recycling (Waste, etc.) 3. Environmental policy.
I. Mancini, Candice.
    TD792.G365 2010
    363.72'8--dc22

                                                                    2010022003

Printed in the United States of America
1 2 3 4 5 6 7 14 13 12 11 10

Contents

Foreword   **11**

Introduction   **14**

Chapter 1: Garbage Issues Throughout the World

1. The World's Oceans Are Filling with Plastic   **21**

   Richard Grant

   Plastic is filling the world's oceans, attracting chemical poisons, killing seabirds and mammals, and ruining beaches. The lump of ocean trash is now twice the size of France, and no one knows how to clean it up.

2. In **India** and Around the World,   **35**
   E-Waste Is Disastrous

   Dataquest

   India generates more than three hundred thousand tons of e-waste each year, and that is expected to multiply several times by 2020.

3. **Americans** Must Be More Responsible   **39**
   with E-Waste

   Chris Jozefowicz

   Each year, Americans throw away millions of electronics, causing toxic chemicals to seep into the earth, the atmosphere, and people's bodies.

4. In **Egypt**, the Nile Is Being Ruined by Pollution   **45**

   Cam McGrath

   Egypt's Nile River is full of pollutants. Studies have found, ironically, that pollution has actually increased numbers of fish, but locals insist that the fish supply is down.

5. In **Serbia**, Garbage and Recycling Must Be   **51**
   a Focus Outside of Belgrade, Too

   Biljana Pavlovic, Amela Bjarovic, Dragan Gmizic, et al.

Belgrade was placed twenty-seventh on a list of thirty green cities in the world, and the rest of Serbia has even more catching up to do.

6. **Bangladesh**'s Capital Is Swimming in Waste   66
Dhaka Courier

India's capital, Bangladesh, generates three thousand to four thousand tons of waste every day: Half is dumped into landfills while the other half is left scattered around the city. The only recycling is done through waste picking.

7. In **Mexico City**, Soon There Will Be No   70
Place to Put Trash
Diego Cevallos

In 2003 and 2004, Mexico City's government promised to clean up the trash, in an environmentally friendly way. The government did not follow through on this promise, and soon there will be nowhere to put trash.

Periodical Bibliography   76

Chapter 2: The Controversial Nature of Garbage and Recycling

1. In the **United Kingdom** and Around the World,   78
People Debate the Value of Recycling
Leo Hickman

Recycling involves much more than tossing the right materials into the right bins. It is a complex system dependent upon the marketplace. Decisions regarding trash disposal are often controversial.

2. In **Canada**, Calgary's Curbside Recycling   93
Sparks Concerns About Recycling
Kevin Libin

Although recycling makes people feel they are helping the environment, excessive recycling does more harm than good.

3. In **India** and **Japan**, Perspectives on   101
Garbage and Recycling Are Different,
but There Is a Common Thread
Urvashi Butalia

Japan's strict garbage and recycling laws may seem severe, especially compared with India's, but they remind us how serious the world's garbage problem is.

4. In **China**, Citizens Protest a Garbage Incinerator Project   107
Wang Pan and Li Jianmin
China's overwhelming garbage problem has sparked the government to build a new garbage incinerator. However, critics of the project claim the incinerator would release carcinogens into the air, causing a health emergency.

5. **China**'s Environmental Mind-Set   114
Gou Fu Mao
An Irishman living in China argues that the Westerners who criticize the Chinese for a lack of environmentalism are the same ones who push a throwaway culture on them. China's environmentalism shines through its professional recyclers who sift through trash.

6. In **South Asia**, Many Ships Meet Their Toxic Death   118
Jacob Baynham
Shipyards of South Asia are full of the toxic ghosts of ancient vessels. Environmental groups are trying to change the vessels' destinies.

Periodical Bibliography   126

Chapter 3: Conventional Solutions to the Garbage and Recycling Dilemma

1. In the **United States** and Around the World, Plastic Bags Must Go   128
Katharine Mieszkowski
The problems with plastic bags are endless: They kill marine life, pollute waters, and, because they do not biodegrade, they never seem to go away.

2. In **Australia**, a Small Town Bans Bottled Water   138
Warren McLaren
Australia's, and possibly the world's, first bottled water–free town has more environmentally friendly ideas on how to distribute drinkable water.

3. In the **United States** and Beyond, Food Service   **144**
   Must Address Waste Management
   Andrew Shakman

   The food service industry has long ignored the importance of good waste management; but it must no longer
   be ignored, for the sake of profits and the environment.

4. In **Spain**, Garbage Management Is Improved   **154**
   Tito Drago

   Spain is incorporating more green-friendly ways to deal
   with the sixty thousand tons of trash it generates daily.

5. In **Canada**, the Package Waste Problem   **160**
   Is Slowly Changing
   Moira Welsh and Christopher Hume

   Largely because of government laws and the now visible
   costs of waste, Canada is slowly emerging out of the
   waste generation crisis.

Periodical Bibliography   **168**

Chapter 4: Alternative Solutions to the Garbage and Recycling Dilemma

1. **American** Architect Turns Trash into Homes   **170**
   Laura Sevier

   American architect Michael Reynolds uses trash to make
   "Earthships," sustainable homes made from recycled garbage and natural materials.

2. In the **Philippines**, Residents Turn Trash   **177**
   into Useful Products
   Ana Puod

   In the Philippines, water lilies clog cities' drainage systems, causing floods. Residents take advantage of the dilemma by turning plants and trash into useful items.

3. In **China** and Beyond, Trash Is Turned into Art   **184**
   PRNewswire-Asia

   Trash is made into art for Expo 2010 in Shanghai, China,
   in order to highlight principles for responsible use of the
   environment.

4. A **British** Entrepreneur Turns Waste into Fuel   **189**
   Danny Fortson
   Philip Hall, a British entrepreneur, is developing technology that could transform trash into fuel, but he is faced
   with skeptics.

5. In **Sweden**, Alcohol and Human Waste Fuel Cars   **194**
   David Wiles
   In a creative twist on recycling, Sweden is turning its
   confiscated booze, feces, and carcasses into fuel.

6. In Space, Recycling Faces New Dilemmas   **199**
   Jon Excell
   Recycling waste is a unique problem for space missions.
   A European-developed processing plant may have a solu-
   tion.

Periodical Bibliography   **204**

For Further Discussion   **205**

Organizations to Contact   **207**

Bibliography of Books   **213**

Index   **216**

Foreword

"The problems of all of humanity can only be solved by all of humanity."
—*Swiss author Friedrich Dürrenmatt*

Global interdependence has become an undeniable reality. Mass media and technology have increased worldwide access to information and created a society of global citizens. Understanding and navigating this global community is a challenge, requiring a high degree of information literacy and a new level of learning sophistication.

Building on the success of its flagship series, *Opposing Viewpoints*, Greenhaven Press has created the *Global Viewpoints* series to examine a broad range of current, often controversial topics of worldwide importance from a variety of international perspectives. Providing students and other readers with the information they need to explore global connections and think critically about worldwide implications, each *Global Viewpoints* volume offers a panoramic view of a topic of widespread significance.

Drugs, famine, immigration—a broad, international treatment is essential to do justice to social, environmental, health, and political issues such as these. Junior high, high school, and early college students, as well as general readers, can all use *Global Viewpoints* anthologies to discern the complexities relating to each issue. Readers will be able to examine unique national perspectives while, at the same time, appreciating the interconnectedness that global priorities bring to all nations and cultures.

Material in each volume is selected from a diverse range of sources, including journals, magazines, newspapers, nonfiction books, speeches, government documents, pamphlets, organization newsletters, and position papers. *Global Viewpoints* is truly global, with material drawn primarily from international sources available in English and secondarily from U.S. sources with extensive international coverage.

Features of each volume in the *Global Viewpoints* series include:

- An **annotated table of contents** that provides a brief summary of each essay in the volume, including the name of the country or area covered in the essay.

- An **introduction** specific to the volume topic.

- A **world map** to help readers locate the countries or areas covered in the essays.

- For each viewpoint, an **introduction** that contains notes about the author and source of the viewpoint explains why material from the specific country is being presented, summarizes the main points of the viewpoint, and offers three **guided reading questions** to aid in understanding and comprehension.

- **For further discussion** questions that promote critical thinking by asking the reader to compare and contrast aspects of the viewpoints or draw conclusions about perspectives and arguments.

- A worldwide list of **organizations to contact** for readers seeking additional information.

- A **periodical bibliography** for each chapter and a **bibliography of books** on the volume topic to aid in further research.

- A comprehensive **subject index** to offer access to people, places, events, and subjects cited in the text, with the countries covered in the viewpoints highlighted.

Global Viewpoints is designed for a broad spectrum of readers who want to learn more about current events, history, political science, government, international relations, economics, environmental science, world cultures, and sociology—students doing research for class assignments or debates, teachers and faculty seeking to supplement course materials, and others wanting to understand current issues better. By presenting how people in various countries perceive the root causes, current consequences, and proposed solutions to worldwide challenges, *Global Viewpoints* volumes offer readers opportunities to enhance their global awareness and their knowledge of cultures worldwide.

Introduction

"Her green plastic watering can
For her fake Chinese rubber plant
In the fake plastic earth
That she bought from a rubber
man
In a town full of rubber plans
To get rid of itself."

Radiohead, "Fake Plastic Trees,"
from The Bends, *1995*

During the 1930s people in the United States and throughout Europe knew the meaning of frugal. The Great Depression was upon them, and resources were scarce. Frugality was vital for all who wanted to eat and have shelter over their heads. People of the 1930s stood by a popular saying: "Use it up, wear it out, make it do or do without." But by the 1950s, frugality was fast becoming old-fashioned, and by the 1980s, developed nations around the globe had mastered the wasteful culture of excessive consumerism. The global financial crisis of the twenty-first century had to sprout from somewhere: Decades of wastefulness were at play. But global economies and household incomes have not been the main casualties of overconsumerism. The environment has taken the biggest hit.

How had it become universal to assume items expire their usefulness after just one use? People of the 1930s would have been incredulous to imagine that societies, en masse, would toss away so much. These include cups, bottles, eating utensils, takeout containers, and the ubiquitous plastic bag, including baggies and grocery bags. On a larger scale are electronics—including washing machines, computers, and radios—which often are thrown away within a few years. How have generations of people grown indifferent to the value of things?

Because of their individual circumstances, our ancestors from the 1930s would have balked at our wastefulness, but environmental responsibility was hardly on the minds of the masses during this time of massive industrialization. The beloved children's author Theodor Geisel, popularly known as Dr. Seuss, who began his writing career in the 1930s, culminated his frustration with environmental irresponsibility in *The Lorax* in 1971. Such sentiments as "Now . . . thanks to your hacking my trees to the ground, there's not enough Truffula Fruit to go 'round," highlight decades of disregard for our earth.

Born in 1904, Dr. Seuss lived through an eventful period spanning the peak of industrialism, the Great Depression, the rise of mass consumption, and the early days of global environmental awareness, the latter of which coincided with the first Earth Day celebration in 1970. As was Dr. Seuss's intent with his pro-environmental, anti-consumerism *The Lorax*, Earth Day was a clear plea for widespread environmental awareness. This plea reached many ears, as demonstrated through the enormous success of Earth Day, even forty years later, and through Universal Studios' decision to transform *The Lorax* into a feature film (scheduled to be released in 2012). But environmental progress is not for the sake of Dr. Seuss or the founder of Earth Day; as a Native American proverb reminds us: "We do not inherit the earth from our ancestors, we borrow it from our children." And much has yet to be done to make amends to our children.

Across the globe every year approximately 500 billion plastic bags are used and tossed out; in the United States alone, people throw away 100 billion plastic bags per year. Plastic grocery bags (as well as water bottles) take up to 1,000 years to decompose; Styrofoam is thought to never decompose. In addition to creating unsightly messes of garbage in landfills and across our natural landscape, plastics and other heaps of waste emit toxic chemicals. These drift into our atmosphere and seep into our ground, affecting air quality, drinking water, crops, fish, and livestock. The toll on marine life alone creates an emergency situation: Up to 1 million sea creatures (including sea turtles, birds, whales and seals) die each year because of millions of discarded plastics in our seas and on our beaches. Plastics also raise the cost of items: In the United States, retailers spend $4 billion a year on plastic bags, which contributes to higher prices. Additionally, plastics are oil hogs: Approximately 60 million barrels of oil are consumed in the world each year just to make plastic bags.

It is obvious that our use of plastics and other resources must be rethought. Environmentalism is not just for tree huggers anymore—it is our inevitable future. If the recent global financial crisis produced anything positive, it is in a global rethinking of the value of goods. Economic woes combined with dwindling resources (most notably oil), pollutants in our food chain and in the atmosphere, and decreasing landfill space make it clear there is only one solution: reduce consumption and produce less waste. Although recycling helps, it is lowest on the resource conservation hierarchy of "reduce, reuse, recycle." Recycling is a good option when an item cannot be reused, but recycling consumes resources, too.

"I think the environment should be put in the category of our national security," said actor and environmental activist Robert Redford at a Yosemite National Park dedication in 1985. "Defense of our resources is just as important as defense abroad. Otherwise what is there to defend?" Even if environmentalism does not reach national security status, sound legislation is needed. For instance, Ireland's 2002 plastic bag tax reduced the use of plastic grocery bags in the country by 94 percent; San Francisco's 2007 ban of any non-compostable plastic grocery bags spread to other towns. But even without legislation, individuals can make small changes that make big differences. Perhaps the easiest way is to refuse the plastic grocery bag. Bringing reusable grocery bags to the store is so simple it is amazing it can make such an impact.

If everyone around the globe brought his or her own bags to stores, instead of using disposable plastic bags, it would save approximately 60 million barrels of oil per year. With approximately 42 gallons of crude oil per barrel, at $80 per barrel, this equates to a savings of 2,520,000,000 gallons of oil and $5,400,000,000 per year. Even if the killing of sea creatures; polluting of air, water, and food; and the ugliness of plastic bags strewn across the landscape is not alarming enough, adding up oil savings over decades might convince a person to bring his or her own bags. While using paper bags eliminates many of the problems associated with plastic, the paper option is responsible for chopping down millions of trees and using its own hefty amount of oil per year.

Plastic water bottles provide similar hazards: In the United States alone, 17 million barrels of crude oil are used to create plastic water bottles each year. This is enough oil to run 1 million cars for a full year. Then there are the chemicals: BPA, a substance found in plastic bottles, is believed to be toxic and to cause a myriad of health problems. Purchasing a BPA-free or steel reusable water bottle, and using tap or filtered water, is easy and can positively affect the environment and your health.

Saying no to unnecessary plastics is an excellent and easy way to start making a difference. Other simple ways to reduce waste include bringing your own containers for leftovers at restaurants (a great way to reuse some of those plastics); buying bulk foods (in your own containers); buying secondhand clothes and organizing clothing swaps with friends; and spreading the word that wastefulness is not cool. By making small changes, individuals can make enormous differences that will lead to a cleaner and less toxic environment; less depletion of natural resources; and better health and well-being of sea life, people, and other living creatures. Unless WALL-E rumbles off the movie screen and into real life, it is up to individuals to lead the way.

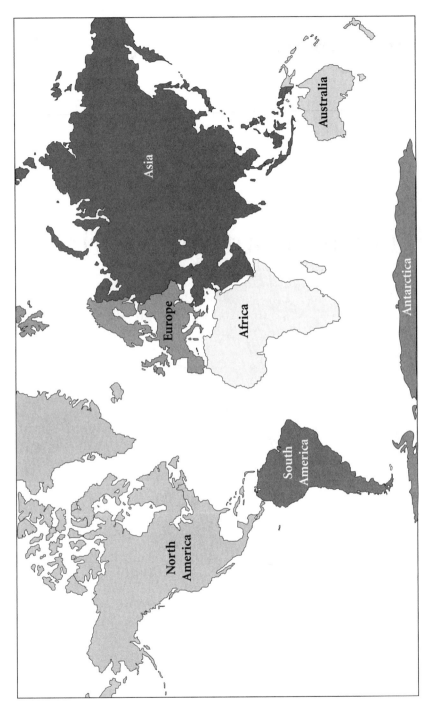

GLOBAL VIEWPOINTS

CHAPTER 1

Garbage Issues
Throughout the World

The World's Oceans Are Filling with Plastic

Richard Grant

Perhaps nothing embodies our state of environmental emergency like the Great Pacific Garbage Patch, a country-sized patch of floating plastic in the Pacific Ocean. In this viewpoint, Richard Grant, a writer for the Telegraph, Reader's Digest, *and other publications, talks with Charles Moore, who discovered the marine soup, as well as others trying to deal with the problem. Moore and others point out that while the plastic cannot be removed from the oceans, people worldwide must stop irresponsibly using and tossing plastics. Others, like David de Rothschild, want to inspire people to creatively cope with the problem.*

As you read, consider the following questions:

1. From where did the Great Pacific Garbage Patch's plastic originate?
2. What dangers do plastic particles present to marine wildlife and to humans?
3. How can industry executives and consumers help manage the plastic problem?

Way out in the Pacific Ocean, in an area once known as the doldrums, an enormous, accidental monument to modern society has formed. Invisible to satellites, poorly understood by scientists and perhaps twice the size of France, the Great Pacific Garbage Patch is not a solid mass, as is sometimes imagined, but a kind of marine soup whose main ingredient is floating plastic debris. It was discovered in 1997 by a Californian sailor, surfer, volunteer environmentalist and early-retired furniture restorer named Charles Moore, who was heading home with his crew from a sailing race in Hawaii, at the helm of a 50ft [foot] catamaran that he had built himself.

For the hell of it, he decided to turn on the engine and take a shortcut across the edge of the North Pacific Subtropical Gyre, a region that seafarers have long avoided. It is a perennial high-pressure zone, an immense, slowly spiralling vortex of warm equatorial air that pulls in winds and turns them gently until they expire. Several major sea currents also converge in the gyre and bring with them most of the flotsam from the Pacific coasts of Southeast Asia, North America, Canada and Mexico. Fifty years ago nearly all that flotsam was biodegradable. These days it is 90 per cent plastic.

'It wasn't a revelation so much as a gradual sinking feeling that something was terribly wrong here.'

From Where Is the Plastic Coming?

'It took us a week to get across and there was always some plastic thing bobbing by,' says Moore, who speaks in a jaded, sardonic drawl that occasionally flares up into heartfelt oratory. 'Bottle caps, toothbrushes, Styrofoam cups, detergent bottles, pieces of polystyrene packaging and plastic bags. Half of it was just little chips that we couldn't identify. It wasn't a revelation so much as a gradual sinking feeling that something was terribly wrong here. Two years later I went back with a fine-mesh net, and that was the real mind-boggling discovery.'

Floating beneath the surface of the water, to a depth of 10 metres [33 feet], was a multitude of small plastic flecks and particles, in many colours, swirling like snowflakes or fish food. An awful thought occurred to Moore and he started measuring the weight of plastic in the water compared to that of plankton. Plastic won, and it wasn't even close. 'We found six times more plastic than plankton, and this was just colossal,' he says. 'No one had any idea this was happening, or what it might mean for marine ecosystems, or even where all this stuff was coming from.'

So ended Moore's retirement. He turned his small volunteer environmental monitoring group into the Algalita Marine Research Foundation, enlisted scientists, launched public awareness campaigns and devoted all his considerable energies to exploring what would become known as the Great Pacific Garbage Patch and studying the broader problem of marine plastic pollution, which is accumulating in all the world's oceans. The world's navies and commercial shipping fleets make a significant contribution, he discovered, throwing some 639,000 plastic containers overboard every day, along with their other litter. But after a few more years of sampling ocean water in the gyre and near the mouths of Los Angeles streams, and comparing notes with scientists in Japan and Britain, Moore concluded that 80 per cent of marine plastic was initially discarded on land, and the United Nations Environment Programme agrees. The wind blows plastic rubbish out of littered streets and landfills, and lorries and trains on their way to landfills. It gets into rivers, streams and storm drains and then rides the tides and currents out to sea. Litter dropped by people at the beach is also a major source.

What Happens to the Plastic?

Plastic does not biodegrade; no microbe has yet evolved that can feed on it. But it does photodegrade. Prolonged exposure to sunlight causes polymer chains to break down into smaller and smaller pieces, a process accelerated by physical friction, such as being blown across a beach or rolled by waves. This accounts for most of the flecks and fragments in the enormous plastic soup at the becalmed heart of the Pacific, but Moore also found a fantastic profusion of uniformly shaped pellets about 2mm [.08 inches] across.

'There's no such thing as a pristine sandy beach anymore.'

Nearly all the plastic items in our lives begin as these little manufactured pellets of raw plastic resin, which are known in the industry as nurdles. More than 100 billion kilograms [over 220 billion pounds] of them are shipped around the world every year, delivered to processing plants and then heated up, treated with other chemicals, stretched and moulded into our familiar products, containers and packaging. During their loadings and unloadings, however, nurdles have a knack for spilling and escaping. They are light enough to become airborne in a good wind. They float wonderfully and can now be found in every ocean in the world, hence their new nickname: mermaids' tears. You can find nurdles in abundance on almost any seashore in Britain, where litter has increased by 90 per cent in the past 10 years, or on the remotest uninhabited Pacific islands, along with all kinds of other plastic confetti.

'There's no such thing as a pristine sandy beach anymore,' Charles Moore says. 'The ones that look pristine are usually groomed, and if you look closely you can always find plastic particles. On Kamilo Beach in Hawaii there are now more plastic particles than sand particles until you dig a foot down. On Pagan Island [between Hawaii and the Philippines] they have what they call the "shopping beach". If the islanders need a cigarette lighter, or some flip-flops, or a toy, or a ball for their kids, they go down to the shopping beach and pick it out of all the plastic trash that's washed up there from thousands of miles away.'

The Ecological Dangers of Plastic

On Midway Island, 2,800 miles west of California and 2,200 miles east of Japan, the British wildlife filmmaker Rebecca Hosking found that many thousands of Laysan albatross chicks are dying every year from eating pieces of plastic that their parents mistake for food and bring back for them.

Worldwide, according to the United Nations Environment Programme, plastic is killing a million seabirds a year, and 100,000 marine mammals and turtles. It kills by entanglement, most commonly in discarded synthetic fishing lines and nets. It kills by choking throats and gullets and clogging up digestive tracts, leading to fatal constipation. Bottle caps, pocket combs, cigarette lighters, tampon applicators, cotton-bud shafts, toothbrushes, toys, syringes and plastic shopping bags are routinely found in the stomachs of dead seabirds and turtles. A study of fulmar carcasses that washed up on North Sea coastlines found that 95 per cent had plastic in their stomachs—an average of 45 pieces per bird.

The Great Pacific Garbage Patch has now been tentatively mapped into an east and west section and the combined weight of plastic there is estimated at three million tons and increasing steadily.

Plastic particles are not thought to be toxic themselves but they attract and accumulate chemical poisons already in the water such as DDT and PCBs [polychlorinated biphenyls]—nurdles have a special knack for this. Plastic has been found inside zooplankton and filter-feeders such as mussels and barnacles; the worry is that these plastic pellets and associated toxins are travelling through the marine food chains into the fish on our plates. Scientists don't know because they are only just beginning to study it.

We do know that whales are ingesting plenty of plastic along with their plankton, and that whales have high concentrations of DDT, PCBs and mercury in their flesh, but that's not proof. The whales could be getting their toxins directly from the water or by other vectors. Research on marine plastic debris is still in its infancy and is woefully underfunded, but we know that there are six major subtropical gyres in the world's oceans—their combined area amounts to a quarter of the earth's surface—and that they are all accumulating plastic soup.

The Paradox of Innovation

The Great Pacific Garbage Patch has now been tentatively mapped into an east and west section and the combined weight of plastic there is estimated at three million tons and increasing steadily. It appears to be the big daddy of them all, but we do not know for sure. Dr Pearn Niiler of the Scripps Institution of Oceanography in San Diego, the world's leading authority on ocean currents, thinks that there is an even bigger garbage patch in the South Pacific, in the vicinity of Easter Island, but no scientists have yet gone to look.

The French cultural theorist Paul Virilio observed that every new technology opens the possibility for a new form of accident. By inventing the locomotive, you also invent derailments. By inventing the aeroplane, you create plane crashes and midair collisions. When Leo Baekeland, a Belgian chemist, started tinkering around in his garage in Yonkers, New York, working on the first synthetic polymer, who could have foreseen that a hundred years later plastic would outweigh plankton six-to-one in the middle of the Pacific Ocean? Baekeland was trying to mimic shellac, a natural polymer secreted by the Asian scale beetle and used at the time to coat electrical wires. In 1909 he patented a mouldable hard plastic that he called Bakelite, and which made him very rich indeed.

Chemists were soon experimenting with variations, breaking down the long hydrocarbon chains in crude petroleum into smaller ones and mixing them together, adding chlorine to get PVC [polyvinyl chloride], introducing gas to get polystyrene. Nylon was invented in 1935 and found its first application in stockings, and then after the Second World War came acrylics, foam rubber, polythene, polyurethane, Plexiglass and more: an incredible outpouring of new plastic products and the revolution of clear plastic food wraps and containers, which preserved food longer and allowed people to live much further away from where it was produced.

Except for the small percentage that has been incinerated, every single molecule of plastic that has ever been manufactured is still somewhere in the environment, and some 100 million tons of it are floating in the oceans.

Single-use plastic bags first appeared in the US [United States] in 1957 and in British supermarkets in the late 1960s; worldwide there are more than a trillion manufactured every year, although the upward trend is now levelling off and falling in many countries, including Britain. We reduced our plastic bag use by 26 per cent last year [2008], to 9.9 billion. Bottled water entered the mass market in the mid-1980s. Global consumption is now 200 billion litres a year and only one in five of those plastic bottles is recycled. The total global production of plastic, which was five million tons in the 1950s, is expected to hit 260 million tons this year.

Look around you. Start counting things made of plastic and don't forget your buttons, the stretch in your underwear, the little caps on the end of your shoelaces. The stuff is absolutely ubiquitous, forming the most basic infrastructure of modern consumer society. We are scarcely out of the womb when we meet our first plastic: wristband, aspirator, thermometer, disposable nappy. We gnaw on plastic teething rings and for the rest of our lives scarcely pass a moment away from plastics. The benefits of plastic, most of which relate to convenience, consumer choice and profit, have been phenomenal. But except for the small percentage that has been incinerated, every single molecule of plastic that has ever been manufactured is still somewhere in the environment, and some 100 million tons of it are floating in the oceans.

A dead albatross was found recently with a piece of plastic from the 1940s in its stomach. Even if plastic production halted tomorrow, the planet would be dealing with its environmental consequences for thousands of years, and on the bottom of the oceans, where an estimated 70 per cent of marine plastic debris ends up—water bottles sink fairly quickly—for tens of thousands of years. It may form a layer in the geological record of the planet, or some microbe may evolve that can digest plastic and find itself supplied with a vast food resource. In the meantime, what can we do?

Finding Creative Ways to Spark Change

What we cannot do is clean up the plastic in the oceans. 'It's the biggest misunderstanding people have on this issue,' Moore says. 'They think the ocean is like a lake and we can go out with nets and just clean it up. People find it difficult to grasp the true size of the oceans and the fact that most of this plastic is in tiny pieces and it's everywhere. All we can do is stop putting more of it in, and that means redesigning our relationship with plastic.'

At the far end of a huge loading warehouse on the San Francisco docks dub reggae is pulsing and two young women are shooting dry ice into two-litre plastic bottles. David de Rothschild, the tall, bearded, long-haired, environmentalist son of the Rothschild banking family, wearing hemp Nikes and a skull-and-bones belt buckle, strides in past a display of nurdles, an aquarium full of plastic soup and various rejected prototypes of the catamaran he intends to build and sail across the Pacific to Australia, visiting the Great Pacific Garbage Patch and various rubbish-strewn islands along the way.

How Big Is 100 Million Tons?

100 million tons of plastic is thought to be floating in the world's oceans. A ton = 2,000 pounds, meaning there are 200 billion pounds of plastic in the oceans.

200 billion pounds is equal to:

- *12 million* elephants
- *142 million* cows
- *1.5 billion* 16- to 18-year-old teens
- *2.5 billion* dogs
- *22 billion* cats
- *28 billion* skateboards
- *200 billion* shoes
- *600 billion* boxes of crayons

Compiled by editor from
http://www.extremescience.com;
http://lifestyle.iloveindia.com;
http://www.petconnection.com;
http://emweb.unl.edu.

He wants the boat to be made entirely out of recycled plastics and float on recycled plastic bottles, and this has presented a daunting challenge to his team of designers, consultants and naval architects. Human ingenuity has devised many fine applications for recycled plastic, but boat-building has not so far been one of them. The design team has had to start from scratch, over and over again. Furthermore, because the point of this voyage is to galvanise media and public attention on the issue of plastic waste, the boat needs to look dramatic and iconic, and it must produce all its own energy, generate no emissions and compost its waste.

'The message of this project is that plastic's not the enemy,' de Rothschild says, speaking rapidly and unstoppably in a mid-Atlantic accent. He is full of bright energy, good humour, marketing slogans and an almost childlike enthusiasm. 'It's about rethinking waste as a resource. It's about doing smart things with plastic and showcasing solutions. It's about using adventure to engage people and start a conversation that creates change in society. You're always going to get people who say, "Oh, he's a bloody Rothschild, sitting on a boat made of, what's that? Champagne bottles?" And that's fine because it gets people talking about it and thinking about where their rubbish goes.'

The idea took hold of him in July 2006. He had just got back from the North Pole, where he led an expedition designed to heighten awareness about global warming. On the Internet he came across a UN [United Nations] report describing the Great Pacific Garbage Patch and estimating that there was now an average of 46,000 pieces of plastic per square kilometre of the world's oceans. 'I thought, this is nuts that we don't know about this! Six-to-one plastic-to-plankton ratio? This has got to be my next expedition.'

An Environmental Marketing Scheme

Born in London, de Rothschild, 31, was a reckless, hyperactive child and teenager who found an outlet for energies in competitive showjumping [competitive horse riding] and triathlons. His school career was erratic but he managed to buckle himself down, pass his A-levels and get into Oxford Brookes University to study computing. Afterwards he got a job with a music licensing and merchandising company, designing Web sites for Britney Spears and U2, and absorbing lasting lessons on the power and strategies of marketing.

Then, with the encouragement of a girlfriend, he got deeply involved in alternative medicine, which led him to organic farming in New Zealand and the subsequent realisation that it was all for naught if the air, the water and the natural environment continued to be poisoned. In 2004 a friend's brother invited him on a 1,150-mile traverse of Antarctica by foot and ski, and on a whim he invited schoolteachers and children in New Zealand to follow the expedition's progress and learn about Antarctica. On his return he founded an organisation, Adventure Ecology, intended to use expeditions to get schoolchildren interested and actively involved in environmental issues. The Arctic global warming expedition was the first. Crossing the Pacific in a recycled-plastic boat will be the second.

He decided to name the boat *Plastiki*, in homage to Kon-Tiki, the raft of balsa logs and hemp ropes in which Thor Heyerdahl sailed across the Pacific in 1947. He recruited designers, a public relations team and corporate sponsors, including Hewlett-Packard and the International Watch Company. He won't say how much it is costing or how much of his own money is going into it, only that it is more than he would like and less than it could be.

Jo Royle, the renowed British yachtswoman, has signed on as skipper, and two of Thor Heyerdahl's grandchildren have agreed to join the crew. And through Adventure Ecology, de Rothschild has launched a competition called SMART, inviting individuals and organisations from science, marketing, art and industrial design research and technology to present tangible solutions to the problems of plastic waste, and offering grants and publicity to the winners.

Ways to Make a Difference

In general terms, it is already clear what we need to do about plastic. Since it is made from oil, which will run out in our lifetimes and get more expensive as it does, we have to start reusing plastic and designing it for reuse. At present only a few of our many hundred plastics can simply be melted down and moulded into something else; the rest are cross-contaminated with other chemicals and types of plastic. But the billion-dollar plastic industry is tooled for virgin plastic and resistant to change. Charles Moore gives talks to plastic industry executives whenever he can and finds very little interest in recycling, because it's the least profitable sector of the industry. 'A lot of companies and product designers and marketing people don't like recycled plastic either,' de Rothschild says, 'You can't dye it with those bright, attention-grabbing colours.'

For consumers, the easiest way to make a difference is to give up plastic shopping bags and plastic water bottles, which contribute more to plastic pollution than any other products. Then comes plastic packaging, which is a little more complicated. It is easy to point out examples of excessive packaging, but plastic does have the virtue of being lighter than paper, cardboard and glass, which gives it a smaller carbon footprint. For food especially, recyclable plastic packaging is probably the best option.

For the hull and cabin of the *Plastiki*, the team was enthused about recycled plastic lumber until they discovered that it sags badly unless reinforced with glass rods. Now they are excited about self-reinforcing PET [polyethylene terephthalate], a new product manufactured in Denmark, similar to fibreglass but fully recycled and recyclable. When heat-fused to boards of PET foam, it appears to be capable of withstanding the battering of Pacific waves for a hundred days, although the effect of salt water on the material is still unknown. Dry ice in the two-litre bottles hardens them without losing any flotation, although some of the bottle caps have managed to work themselves loose and are now being resealed with what de Rothschild calls 'a very cool bio-glue' made from cashew nuts and sugar.

Reshifting Priorities

Sitting now with a pint of beer and an artichoke in a restaurant opposite the waterfront, he is confident that the *Plastiki* will be built and on its way to Australia some time this summer. 'We do need to get from A to B but what this project is really about is remarketing and rebranding the message about recycling, about sustainability, about interconnectedness,' he says. What he sees as the failure of the environmental movement, as measured by ever-increasing carbon emissions, rain forest destruction, species extinctions and marine plastic debris, he understands as a failure of marketing and communication, rather than insurmountable forces working in the opposite direction.

'To effect change, you've got to inspire people, not moan at them.'

'The environmental message has been very exclusive, very guilt-mongering, very fear-mongering, and is that the right way to engage with people? We're bombarded by 2,500 images a day. How are you going to stop someone watching *Lost* and make them watch someone saying, "You're a bad person because you don't drive a hybrid"? To effect change, you've got to inspire people, not moan at them.'

After another pint, he admits to serious doubts—not that the *Plastiki* will get built and complete its voyage, but that it is still possible to save the oceans from ecological collapse. Overfishing is the most urgent problem, but what really scares him and the marine scientists is acidification caused by global warming. The oceans are absorbing more and more of the carbon dioxide that we are putting into the air and it is changing the pH [measure of acidity and alkalinity] of the water, turning the seas more acid, with potentially catastrophic effects on marine organisms and ecosystems.

'A lot of scientists think we're basically screwed, but what are you going to do?' he asks. 'Enjoy your beer, enjoy your family, make the most of it while it lasts? I think there's a real big movement for that at the moment and part of me understands that. But there's a bigger part of me that says we've got to find a solution, collectively. I mean, come on. We spent $265 billion preparing for the Y2K [year 2000] bug and we didn't even know if it was going to happen or not. We know for an absolute fact that if we continue on our current rate of consumption, we're going to run out of resources. But the annual budget for the United Nations Environment Programme last year was $190 million. And the budget for the latest James Bond movie was $205 million.'

He chuckles at that, checks his watch and calls for the bill. It is time to walk the dogs and then work the second half of his standard 17-hour day. Outside, he points to San Francisco Bay, looking pristine and lovely in the late afternoon sunshine. 'Maybe that's the trouble,' he says. 'You'd never guess what's under the surface if you didn't know, would you?'

In India and Around the World, E-Waste Is Disastrous

Dataquest

Dataquest is India's oldest information technology publication. In the following viewpoint, Dataquest *reports on the status of e-waste disposal and recycling in India. Only about 10 percent of the e-waste is recycled per year, and India also has tons of e-waste imported illegally each year. The prospect for the next ten years is for e-waste in India to increase 500 percent from the 2007 level.*

As you read, consider the following questions:

1. How many tons of hazardous waste did India generate in 2007?
2. How many tons of e-waste did India generate in 2007?
3. How many tons of e-waste does India import each year?

Everyone is so lost in the urban rat race that we all have forgotten the world around us. We never stop and think about what we are giving back to the earth other than the increased carbon footprints and e-wastes. We have all the bad things to highlight if we start analyzing from carbon emissions to e-wastes.

According to a UN [United Nations] report, India is the second largest e-waste generator in Asia. Unless action is taken

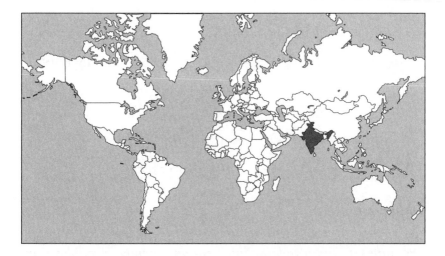

immediately to properly collect and recycle materials, many developing countries will face the specter of hazardous e-waste mountains with serious consequences regarding the environment and public health, the report warns. In the year 2009, India generated 5.9 mn [million] tonnes of hazardous waste, posing serious health issues.

The UN study says that by 2020, e-wastes from old computers would jump by 500% from the 2007 levels in India, and by 200% to 400% in South Africa and China. The e-wastes from old mobile phones will be seven times higher in China and eighteen times higher in India.

The e-wastes from old mobile phones will be seven times higher in China and eighteen times higher in India [in 2020 than in 2007].

A recent report by the Delhi-based Centre for Science and Environment (CSE) says that apart from generating about 3,50,000 tonnes of electronic waste every year, India imports another 50,000 tonnes. The study alleges that the unorganized sector recycles more than 90% of this; and instead of organizing this sector, government chooses to ignore it.

A Destructive Trade

The export of toxic wastes to poorer economies for recycling is an unacceptable transfer of pollution to those least able to afford it. It can only be justified by brute economics and not from a moral or environmental standpoint. Such trade leaves the workers in developing countries with a choice between poverty and poison—a choice nobody should have to make. Moreover, by allowing a convenient escape valve for rich consumptive societies and manufacturers, it stifles the innovation needed to truly solve our toxic waste problems through upstream "green" design and clean production. We must all do our part to reaffirm the Basel Convention [on the Control of Transboundary Movements of Hazardous Wastes and Their Disposal] commitment to ban this destructive trade.

Basel Action Network,
"Turn Back the Toxic Tide," Briefing Paper 7,
June 2008. www.ban.org.

The organization also says that Attero Recycling which has the only license in India to import e-waste is reselling e-waste instead of recycling it. It is illegally trading e-waste, and such illegal trade results in huge pollution in the industry. As per the data, India generated 3,30,000 tonnes of e-waste in 2007 which is equal to 110 mn laptops. About 10% of the e-waste generated is recycled every year; the remaining is refurbished, and the unorganized sector is right behind almost all of it. Informal dealers refurbish and make money from e-waste.

According to CSE, the governments new draft rules with regard to waste management ignore the reality and are likely to be toothless. It is estimated that illegal import of e-waste in the country stands at about 50,000 tonnes annually and loopholes in the laws facilitate this. "We need to think how we can build a new model for waste managers. Instead of thinking about replacing small, cost-effective garbage collectors with big business, we have to think how policy can legalize, regulate and even pay for this trade to happen not out of sight, but under our noses," says Sunita Narain, director, CSE.

It is being reported that the free trade agreements currently being negotiated with the European Union and Japan include provisions for these countries to dump their e-waste in India. If this trend continues, India will soon become the dumping ground for global e-waste. It's our duty to prevent such a global disaster.

Americans Must Be More Responsible with E-Waste

Chris Jozefowicz

Chris Jozefowicz is a science writer living in New York City. In the following viewpoint, Jozefowicz points out that around the globe, billions of tons of e-waste—including TVs, cell phones, computers, and printers—get thrown out every year. Very few of these items are recycled, and among the biggest contributors to the e-waste problem, he contends, are Americans. Jozefowicz notes that e-waste is highly toxic, which is especially problematic because the United States and other wealthy nations ship their e-waste to poorer nations, intoxicating those populations and the environment with poisons. He urges people to be more responsible in their buying and recycling of electronics.

As you read, consider the following questions:

1. According to Greg Spears, what percentage of appliances can be recycled?
2. What do people in poorer countries do with the e-waste that is shipped to them?
3. What four substances does the Environmental Protection Agency deem as especially dangerous?

Matthew Gallagher has skeletons in his attic—and stuffed into a drawer. The 19-year-old from Louisville, Ky., is holding on to the skeletons of electronics past. His family has

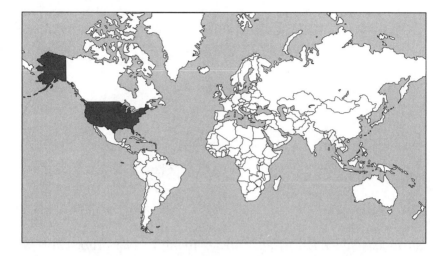

an old TV and a computer in the attic. Gallagher keeps an ob-
solete MP3 player and a collection of abandoned handheld
games in a drawer.

While the old electronics languish, Gallagher is dreaming
of new gadgets. "Oh, I definitely want to upgrade," he says. He
hopes to get a new smart phone and a laptop computer during his first year of college. So why keep the old stuff? "Sub-
consciously, I guess I think I'll use them again," admits Gallagher. But he rarely does. Instead, they pile up as electronic
waste, or e-waste, inside the Gallagher house.

E-waste is junk with significant electronic components.
"Basically, it is anything with a circuit board," says Barbara
Kyle, the national coordinator for the Electronics TakeBack
Coalition, an organization that fights e-waste. Electronic
equipment contains chemicals that can be dangerous if people
come in contact with them. Yet tons of electronics are thrown
away each day. Some companies even ship e-waste to other
countries, where it may be taken apart by people for little
money and with a big risk of damage to their health. "The
problem is growing exponentially," says Kyle. "Think about all
the stuff we have that wasn't even around five years ago."

Trash in the Twenty-First Century

Some consumers, such as the Gallagher family, hoard old equipment. But most electronics end up as part of the waste stream. In 2007, Americans discarded 2.5 million tons of TVs, cell phones, computers, and printers, according to the Environmental Protection Agency (EPA). Worldwide, people throw away 10 to 20 times as much each year. That's enough e-waste to fill a train that stretches around the globe.

A fraction of those electronics gets recycled. Greg Spears is vice president of American Industrial Services, an Indiana company involved in recycling e-waste. "We're seeing a lot of TVs because of the switch over to digital TV" last year [2009], he says. Recyclers break down electronics and separate the plastic, metal, glass, and other parts to reuse. Spears estimates that 90 percent of appliances, such as TVs or computer monitors, can be recycled.

But EPA figures suggest that more than 80 percent of electronics in the United States are not recycled. Some of those electronics end up in landfills close to home. Many more are shipped overseas—sometimes illegally—and left in huge e-waste dumps in Asia, Africa, and Latin America.

Chemicals can leach into the ground, water, or air if e-waste is not disposed of properly. Professor Valerie Thomas studies recycling at the Georgia Institute of Technology in Atlanta. She says dangerous chemicals are the biggest problem related to e-waste. . . . "E-waste contains chemicals that are toxic," Thomas says. "It can pollute if it goes into a landfill or incinerator, and it can pollute if it is recycled because it has to be opened up."

So why would other countries take dangerous waste? For money, of course. Spears says junk can often be shipped overseas for less money than it takes to dismantle and sell the parts in the United States. Poor people living in countries such as China or Ghana will then break apart the old electronics and sell the parts for a few dollars a day. Often, children work beside adults in the e-waste scrap yards. In most cases, laws to protect those workers are weak or nonexistent.

"The electronics land in places where people earn next to nothing," Kyle says. "The system relies on low-wage workers to basically bash open electronics. People remove the metals and junk the rest. They burn the plastics. It's literally poisoning people."

Those old, thick TVs that are being replaced by flat-screen models can contain more than 5 pounds of lead in each screen. The lead may poison workers who break apart the TVs, and it often pollutes the environment around e-waste dumps. More than 80 percent of kids living in one e-waste recycling town in China had high levels of lead in their blood, according to a recent study. That's a huge health problem because elevated lead levels can damage nerves and kidneys, and slow bone and muscle growth. Lead is particularly dangerous for kids' brains, which are still developing. Additional studies have shown that people who live and work near e-waste dumps have high levels of other dangerous chemicals in their bodies, raising the risk for cancer and a range of other diseases.

Responsible Buying and Recycling

To prevent e-waste pollution from spreading, people in countries that generate millions of tons of waste—such as the United States—must work to recycle responsibly. Many communities have e-waste recycling collections, but people still need to call the recycler to make sure their e-waste is not shipped overseas. Some large store chains offer free recycling for old electronics and batteries. Even the U.S. Postal Service runs a program that allows people to mail small electronics to a recycler free of charge.

Kyle and the Electronics TakeBack Coalition want the federal government to pass laws forbidding the export of e-waste to other nations. "We think manufacturers should take back and recycle our old products when we are done with them, and that the price of the products should include the cost of recycling," Kyle says. "Otherwise, people pay for it [with their health] in China."

Young people buy and use so many electronic gadgets that they have the power to influence better e-waste practices.

Consumers can also help solve e-waste problems by buying electronics made with fewer toxic chemicals. . . . Everyone should keep some simple goals in mind to help reduce waste in their electronics, Thomas says. "People should ask themselves, 'Can I upgrade my old one instead of getting a new one? How long will this product last?'"

Young people buy and use so many electronic gadgets that they have the power to influence better e-waste practices. One such activist is Jennifer Roberts, who helped fight e-waste at the University of California (UC) in Santa Cruz, where she was recently a student. She helped create Toxic Free UC, a group that succeeded in inspiring the university to commit to buying electronics that are low in toxins and easy to recycle.

"Students can make their own campaigns," Roberts says. "There has to be a grassroots campaign of consumers. People have to say, 'I'm not going to support your company if you are putting all these horrible chemicals in your computers and cell phones and not taking care of them at the end of their lives.'"

A Greener Future

E-waste would disappear if companies could use "green design" techniques to make recyclable electronics without any toxic components. Right now, that is impossible, but researchers such as Valerie Thomas are dreaming of that day. Thomas, a professor at the Georgia Institute of Technology, explores ways people might make recycling easier. "Could computers be designed so that they are as environmentally benign as a cardboard box?" she asks.

Some computer companies have pledged to remove chemicals such as brominated flame retardants from their products to make them safer. Environmental groups and consumers keep up the pressure for even safer products. Thomas predicts that more people would recycle electronics when all they had to do was put them out with the rest of their recycling in a pickup bin. Instead of tossing your old computer or cell phone in the trash, what could you do to keep them from becoming e-waste?

Instead of tossing your old computer or cell phone in the trash, what could you do to keep them from becoming e-waste?

"Electronics are where a lot of toxins live," says Barbara Kyle from the Electronics TakeBack Coalition. People who use products normally are at little risk of exposure. But if electronic equipment is not taken care of at the end of its life—if it is broken or disposed of improperly—the chemicals can escape into the environment. The following four substances are singled out by the Environmental Protection Agency as particularly dangerous: [lead, mercury, brominated flame retardants, and cadmium.]

In Egypt, the Nile Is Being Ruined by Pollution

Cam McGrath

The Nile River, which has long been a major source of sustenance for Egyptians, is in danger. In this viewpoint, Cam McGrath, a Canadian journalist based in Cairo, discusses how pollution is destroying the Nile and making it dangerous to bathe in, drink from, or eat fish that has been caught there. Those who use the Nile are suffering from kidney problems, skin irritations, and other health problems. He reports that declining numbers of fish have also been attributed to pollution, but officials claim overfishing—not pollution—has led to fewer fish.

As you read, consider the following questions:

1. According to the viewpoint, what are the three main sources of pollution in the Nile River?
2. According to Malcolm Beveridge, which source of pollution should cause the most concern?
3. Paradoxically, what has the large-scale dumping of sewage and fertilizers into the Nile done to fish populations, according to researchers?

After four hours on the Nile in a rowboat with his two sons, fisher Hussein Abdel Malek tallies the morning catch: a plastic water bottle, an empty juice box, a half dozen plastic bags and two small tilapia.

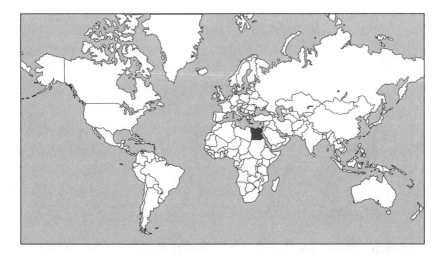

"The fish were sleeping today," he jests.

It has been years since the fish were 'awake', and even Abdel Malek's sanguine humour cannot hide his disappointment. He has been fishing the ancient river since he was old enough to walk and reckons he's spent more of his life on his six-metre-long wooden skiff than he has on dry land.

> *"The river used to be much cleaner. . . . There was no floating garbage and you could see lots of fish swimming near shore."*

Pollution and overfishing have decimated Nile fish stocks, he asserts. In his youth, a basketful of fish could be caught in a few hours. Now he spends an entire day just to catch a few fish.

"The river used to be much cleaner," Abdel Malek says. "There was no floating garbage and you could see lots of fish swimming near shore."

The Nile's Sources of Pollution

The vast majority of Egypt's 80 million inhabitants live along the banks of the Nile. The river, which enters the country near the southern city of Aswan, flows 1,300 kilometres before emptying into the Mediterranean Sea near Alexandria.

"You can drink the Nile near Aswan, but by the time the water reaches Cairo it is heavily polluted," says Sherif Sadek, a former fisheries official. "Some species could not tolerate the polluted water and are no longer found in the river."

A report issued by Egypt's environment ministry in September [2009] identified three main sources of Nile pollution as untreated sewage, agricultural drainage, and industrial effluents. It said the country produces an estimated 12 million cubic metres of wastewater a day, of which a large portion is discharged into the Nile.

"Domestic wastewater collected from approximately 5,000 basins in small remote villages (is) directly discharged into agricultural drains without treatment, in addition to the untreated or secondary treated sewage from sanitation networks of major cities," the report says.

"The river is basically Egypt's sewer and I wouldn't eat anything living in it."

Agricultural runoff, including an unspecified amount of fertilisers and pesticides, enters the Nile through 75 major drainages, according to the report. Over 100 industrial complexes discharge a total of four billion cubic metres of effluents into the river each year. Other sources of pollution include houseboats and thousands of motorised river vessels.

While authorities who monitor the river insist that pollution levels are within permissible limits, many Egyptians are concerned about the effect of contaminants on the river's fish.

"The river is basically Egypt's sewer and I wouldn't eat anything living in it," says Mona Radwan, a marketing agent who lives in an upscale Cairo neighbourhood. "Many Egyptians eat fish from the Nile because they are too poor to afford meat or chicken."

Africa's Growing Water Problem Must Be Faced

In Egypt and throughout Africa, residents are facing serious water pollution problems that endanger their health and livelihood.

- 13% of the world's population lives in Africa.

- 14% of African countries are currently facing water stress.

- By 2025, 50% of Africa's population of approximately 1.45 billion people will struggle to find clean water.

- 650 Africans (mostly children) die from diarrhea, an ailment directly linked to water pollution, every day.

Group2WP,
The African Water Experience Proposal,
November 13, 2009. http://group2wp.greenpress.com.

Experts say it is important to differentiate between organic and inorganic pollutants.

"With human waste, the principal concern is parasite and disease cycles, but I don't think there's much evidence to show that fish feeding (on sewage) pose a risk to human health, particularly if the fish are cooked properly before they are eaten," says Malcolm Beveridge of the Malaysia-based World-Fish Center. "A bigger concern might be industrial and agricultural wastes, especially heavy metals and toxic pesticides."

The Paradoxical Effect of Pollution

Among the highest at risk are the 15,000 fishermen who drink, bathe in, and eat fish from the Nile. Many suffer from kidney problems, skin irritations and bilharzia, a waterborne parasite.

Abdel Malek worries more about his family's declining income than his chronic kidney pain. He earns between two and eight dollars a day depending on how full his nets are. His sons help row, and swim in the river to scare fish into the nets. His wife sells the catch at a local market and to riverside restaurants.

"There are less fish now, of that I am certain," Abdel Malek says. "There are days when we catch nothing at all."

The consensus among fishermen is that the Nile's fish stocks are declining. Officials, however, insist the river's productivity is higher than ever. They argue that the perception of a declining fish population is due to the increasing number of fishers competing for resources and localized pockets of overfishing near urban centres.

Beveridge says the Nile's fish population declined sharply after completion of the Aswan High Dam in the 1960s, but has rebounded in recent years.

"Studies have shown that fish production collapsed in the second half of the 1960s, because the dam trapped organically rich sediment that the delta, and indeed large areas of the eastern Mediterranean, were dependent upon for fish productivity," he told IPS [Inter Press Service].

"But then something very peculiar happened. In the 1980s fish production began to increase again, and today yields are higher than they were before the high dam's construction."

A team of U.S. and Egyptian researchers found that the massive dumping of sewage and fertilisers into the river had increased concentrations of nitrogen and phosphorous, in the water, stimulating fish growth. In a study published last January in the Proceedings of the National Academy of Sciences, they concluded that these anthropogenic nutrients had offset the river's organic nutrient loss, contributing to a three-fold increase in fish landings over pre-dam levels.

While the research was based on fisheries of the Nile delta's coastal waters, its conclusions have been extrapolated to the river itself. Artificial nutrient enrichment may have inadvertently reversed declining fish stocks, but the study's authors warn that pollution is not a solution.

"Some preliminary evidence indicates that increasing nutrient loads may stimulate (fish) landings up to a point, beyond which the fisheries decline due to poor water quality or overfishing," they say.

In Serbia, Garbage and Recycling Must Be a Focus Outside of Belgrade, Too

Biljana Pavlovic, Amela Bjarovic, Dragan Gmizic, et al.

In this viewpoint, Biljana Pavlovic and other journalists paint a dire picture of waste management in Serbia: Garbage is a common sight throughout the landscape, polluting rivers and releasing poisonous gases into the air. Nearly 40 percent of household waste winds up in unlicensed and unregulated landfills, and there is no immediate end in sight. According to the authors, constraints of politics, finances, and established habits regarding trash have gotten in the way of change. New habits regarding waste must be embraced, they urge.

As you read, consider the following questions:

1. Why must health inspectors sometimes close down registered dumps?

2. What are the objectives of companies involved in Serbia's National Strategy for Waste Management?

3. What are some of the trash problems faced in areas outside of major cities, such as in southern Serbia?

Biljana Pavlovic, Amela Bjarovic, Dragan Gmizic, et al. "Serbia Takes Slow Road to Cleaning Up Waste," *BalkanInsight.com*, January 5, 2010. Copyright © 2010 Balkan Investigative Reporting Network. This article originally appeared in *Balkan Insight*, *www.BalkanInsight.com*, a product of the Birn Serbia Training and Reporting Programme, supported by the National Endowment for Democracy, NED. Reproduced by permission.

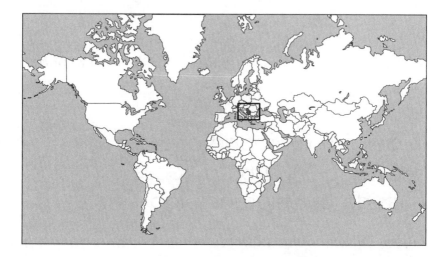

Serbia is far from establishing an ecologically safe and efficient system of managing communal waste, half of which still ends up in unregulated landfills, endangering environment and people alike.

At the conference on global warming in Copenhagen, which was the centre of world attention in December [2009], the Economist Intelligence Unit, monitoring 30 cities, put Belgrade in unflattering 27th place on its list of green cities.

Belgrade is just a microcosm of the whole country, however, where garbage is strewn everywhere, rivers are polluted and dumps release noxious gases into the air.

Serbia is one of the last European countries not to have a market for communal waste.

According to official data, 40 per cent of household waste finishes up in as many as 4,400 unlicenced and unregulated landfill sites. In some areas, epidemics break out, resulting in health inspectors closing down even registered, official dump sites.

Delays in adopting necessary laws and bylaws, inefficiency on the part of the local and central authorities, financial shortages and complicated bureaucratic procedures are some reasons why Serbia is near to the bottom of the chart of European countries when it comes to efficient garbage disposal.

Serbia is one of the last European countries not to have a market for communal waste. There is little attempt to recycle or separate waste into its component parts. Attempts to bring the private sector into the field of waste management have not necessarily been successful, either. Connecting up municipalities in order to build joint regional landfills has proved difficult to implement, and many questions remain about the way landfills might work in the future.

Challenges to Cleanup Strategies

Serbia adopted a "National Strategy for Waste Management", which promoted the concept of regional sanitary landfills, back in 2003. The concept envisages smaller municipalities jointly forming companies whose task is to independently, or in tandem with the private sector, manage communal waste. Together, the municipalities must have a minimum of 200,000 citizens.

The companies would build regional landfills to store household waste, and refuse from public spaces, industrial production and transport that does not contain dangerous substances.

Such landfills must meet strict ecological standards, protecting nearby land and water from further pollution and controlling gas emissions. Uncontrolled burning of waste would be banned.

However, of the 29 regional landfills envisaged in the strategy, only two have been built. As for the construction of recycling, or natural gas–collecting plants in the landfills—another part of the strategy—that remains a far-off goal.

Serbia's Minister of Environment and Spatial Planning, Oliver Dulic, admits that work on the strategy is not proceeding as fast as it might. "Regulations were not adopted and implementation was not [originally] made obligatory," he explained. . . . Implementation of the strategy only became obligatory after parliament adopted the new act on waste management in May 2009.

Dulic says that some progress has been achieved in the meantime through the ministry's own action project, "Let's Clean Up Serbia". There is a plan to cut the number of unregulated landfills by 60 per cent by 2010. Such measures would certainly help redeem Serbia's tarnished ecological image—if new unregulated landfills do not emerge in the meantime.

Serbia has seen sharp growth in the amount of communal waste generated per person lately. An average citizen produced 620 grams of waste daily in 2006, and 950 grams in 2008—a rise of one-third in two years. The total amount of generated waste annually grew from 1.73 million tons in 2006 to 2.55 million tons in 2008. Since official data says only 1.52 million tons of waste was collected in 2008, it is clear that over a million tons of waste ended up that year in unregulated landfills.

Dulic says one way to tackle this is to boost the number of properties receiving waste collection services to 75 per cent by 2013. "We will construct 24 regional centres for waste management in two stages, till 2018," the minister added. "This means the construction of regional landfills, plants to select and separate recyclable waste and plants for biological treatment of waste . . . in each region," he continued.

The ministry expects a breakthrough to become visible by 2010. But experience so far suggests many traps lie ahead. Difficult choices facing municipalities, over whether to leave waste collection and management to private partners, manage the issue through a joint enterprise or keep the job to themselves are only some of the obstacles.

The City Dilemma

The largest urban concentrations in Serbia, Belgrade, Novi Sad and Nis, not surprisingly produce most waste. Yet the capital [Belgrade], with a population of 2 million, has only a single landfill. And even this landfill is not regulated according to European ecological standards.

The authorities in Belgrade have not come up with a waste management strategy, or taken a clear stance on whether to construct one or more regional landfills.

The job of gathering and managing waste in Belgrade is currently done by Gradska Cistoca, a public company that covers 10 Belgrade municipalities with around half a million households. Gradska Cistoca daily collects and stores around 1,500 tons of waste, which then goes to 65-hectare landfill in Vinca, in use since 1977.

Asked why Belgrade has done so little to improve its waste management, the city's environment chief, Goran Trivan, puts most blame on the previous municipal administration, adding that 2010 would see evidence of progress. "A new act has been adopted and now we will solve everything through that strategy, including how many landfills are required and how we're going to build them," he said.

"We know we need a sanitary technical landfill with a modern recycling centre."

Belgrade's waste problems have attracted attention from foreign investors who have shown interest in taking over the landfill in Vinca under a 25-year concession. In 2006 and 2007, the then city manager, the city's chief administrative officer, Bojan Stanojevic, announced that a tender would be organised and although some initial work was undertaken, the process did not come to fruition.

Authorities in Novi Sad, capital of the northern province of Vojvodina, home to 280,000 people, have done little better.

Lidija Tomas, head of management for communal affairs, says most of 2009 was spent analysing the new waste law and by-law documentation. No definite decision on constructing a modern landfill would be made until 2010.

"We know we need a sanitary technical landfill with a modern recycling centre. What we still don't know is which municipalities will partner up with us and whether a private company would be involved," [said] Tomas. . . .

Unofficial talks are under way with neighbouring municipalities, as well as with interested foreign and local companies, she added. For the meantime, all the waste in Novi Sad is still taken to the old landfill, which has numerous shortcomings.

Nis, the largest city in central Serbia, with a population of over 250,000, only began addressing problems over waste management in 2009 when a plan was drafted to construct a regional landfill.

The city also plans to repair the existing landfill, built in the 1950s and closed by sanitary inspectors on several occasions as a health hazard. The mayor, Milos Simonovic, has set a five-year deadline to close the existing unhygienic landfill and set up a regional waste management centre.

"Several authorities before this one promised to repair the landfill but no one provided the money," [said] Sanja Popovic, chair of the city's council for environmental protection. . . . Popovic said this had now changed. They had, he said, received some funding from the government's "Fund for Environmental Protection" and had secured a $100,000 grant from the MEGA [Municipal Economic Growth Activity] programme of USAID [United States Agency for International Development] to draft a regional plan for waste management.

The future regional landfill will cover a wide area with a total population of around 400,000, embracing the municipalities of Gadzin Han, Merosina, Svrljig, Aleksinac and Sokobanja.

"We will have considerable amounts of waste which could be interesting for both recycling and energy use," Popovic said. "Several foreign companies have presented projects to Nis but our goal is to first draw up a financial analysis and only then decide how and with whom to use the waste," Popovic added.

Problems with the Private Sector

Dilemmas over which model to choose worry many local authorities. Many recognise there is potential in charging for some services, in recycling and in using waste to generate energy.

While some authorities have secured financing to modernise their waste services themselves, others have left the job to foreign companies through joint investments or concessions.

Minister Dulic says the participation of the private sector can be categorised three ways: the participation in which the public sector remains the owner of funds and is responsible for investment and the risks are shared; concessions where the right of management is entrusted to the private sector through a contract but ownership is retained; privatisation, full or partial.

"The Fund for Environmental Protection, as well as international financial institutions, is co-financing the construction of regional landfills," Dulic said.

Practice, meanwhile, so far has shown that municipalities have become involved in regional landfill projects, either with the aid of local or international donors or in partnership with international waste management companies—but in most cases, only those municipalities working with foreign business partners have fully complete and operating sites.

The participation of the private sector is not always successful. One such example comes from Kikinda, in Vojvodina, a municipality home to around 70,000 people, where an Austrian company, A.S.A Internacional, built a 26-hectare regional landfill in 2008 with enough capacity to dispose of communal waste for the next 50 years.

The municipality and A.S.A Internacional formed a joint company with a plan to dispose of, store and later sort and press the collected waste of several neighbouring municipalities. But after construction of the landfill in 2008, further progress halted.

Both the municipality and A.S.A accuse each other of failing to meet contractual obligations. On one side, the municipality is late in paying for waste storage and has failed to attract partners among any of the six municipalities initially interested. On the other, A.S.A has not launched the selection and recycling sides of the project, as the contract stipulated.

The head of Kikinda's municipal management, Branko Ljuboja, says the municipalities of Ada, Novi Becej, Becej, Zitiste, Nova Crnja, Coka and Novi Knezevac still have not agreed on how and where to store their waste. "It is very hard to motivate them to join the project since they do not have enough money to pay for it," Ljuboja explained.

A.S.A's manager for Serbia, Ljubomir Niksic, meanwhile dismisses claims that A.S.A has not met its obligations. "The tender that A.S.A won . . . was organised for a market of 140,000 people and plans were prepared in accordance with that," he said. "But while the municipalities at an early stage signed protocols and agreements, this has still not happened."

To complicate matters, a trial is now ongoing against Kikinda's former mayor, Branislav Blazic, who signed the contract with A.S.A and who is charged with damaging the municipality by almost 130 million dinars [approximately $1.8 million], amid claims that A.S.A Internacional got the contract in violation of the criteria for public tenders. Both Blazic and A.S.A deny the accusations.

Despite the problems in Vojvodina, A.S.A in October 2009 opened [another] landfill in Serbia, in Lapovo, in the Sumadija area. This has been more successful. Waste from five municipalities will be disposed here for the next 25 years. However, the regional landfill in Lapovo is only a place for waste disposal. There are no facilities to recycle or collect gas. "In order to produce energy at a landfill, it is first necessary to exploit the landfill for three to five years," explained Niksic.

Lapovo's mayor, Dragan Zdravkovic, [explained] . . . that the main motive for becoming involved with a strategic partner was economic. "We could never afford to buy 21 hectares [approximately 52 acres], which is the size of the landfill, and besides the land there were other expenses we could not cover alone," he said. The ownership structure in the joint company is 51 to 49 in favour of A.S.A, the mayor added.

Politics Get in the Way

Novi Pazar, the main town in the Sandzak region of southwest Serbia, is an example of a municipality where change of power has resulted in a radical change of stance towards regional landfill management.

After the . . . elections in 2008, . . . [the] town . . . broke off the existing contract with a foreign partner and decided to establish a waste disposal system and regional landfill on its own. Municipal heads [said] they acted on fears of a hostile public reaction to possible price rises for communal services, likely job losses in local communal services, and out of awareness that waste disposal is potentially lucrative.

Back in September 2007, the city assembly entrusted the construction of a recycling centre to Lemna International, from Minneapolis in the US [United States]. The contract obliged the company to take on all the workers from the existing company and build the recycling centre and landfill. The municipality was obliged to provide and lease the land.

The then city manager, Esad Salihovic, [explained] that Novi Pazar had been the first town in Serbia to embrace the

Greenest Cities in Europe

In its first European Green City Index, Siemens AG presented a list of Europe's greenest cities at the 2009 UN Climate Change Conference in Copenhagen. Judging criteria included CO_2 emissions; energy; buildings; transportation; water; air quality; waste and land use; and environmental governance. The top 5 greenest European cities were:

TAKEN FROM: "European Green City Index," Siemens AG. http://www .siemens.com/press/en/events/corporate/2009-12-cop15.php.

concept of recycling, and of building a sanitary landfill using foreign knowledge, technology and money.

However, the new town management cancelled the contract and started drafting a feasibility study for a regional landfill, to be used by Novi Pazar, Raska, Tutin and Sjenica. A representative of the town's waste disposal services, Osman Hamidovic, said this had proved a better solution, because citizens would pay less. The head of the Department of Local Economic Development, Edin Kalac, says the whole job could be completed in three to four years.

Meanwhile the town is still disposing of its waste at the old landfill, 20 kilometres [approximately 12 miles] from town, which does not operate according to modern ecological standards. A large proportion of garbage is also dumped in unregulated landfills and rivers, the secretary general of a local NGO [nongovernmental organisation], Raskin Sliv, Ibrahim Mehmedovic, explained.

"There are a lot of unregulated landfills and their number often changes," he [said] "They are usually the work of private butchers from Novi Pazar who throw their animal bones onto the roadside or into woods because the landfill is too far away."

"There are a lot of unregulated landfills and their number often changes."

Uzice in western Serbia also took a political decision not to build a landfill with a foreign partner, but in cooperation with neighbouring municipalities. Profits were not the only motive but the confusing regulations in effect before adoption of the new law.

In 1998 Uzice planned a regional landfill at Duboko. Belgrade company Hemko was charged with drawing up plans for the facility. Along with Uzice, eight other towns, Bajina Basta, Pozega, Arilje, Cajetina, Kosjeric, Lucani, Ivanjica and Cacak, additionally planned to use the site.

The Duboko regional public communal company was founded in October 2005 and soon attracted attention of foreign companies from Israel, Germany, Austria, Hungary and the US.

Milomir Sredojevic, then deputy mayor when the company was founded, says the location for the landfill had already been provided for. But with the project cost at 12 million euros [approximately $16 million], it had been necessary to find extra financing.

"This [waste disposal] is currently the fourth or fifth business in the world, so it attracted foreign companies to come and present themselves to us," he recalls. "Partnership was discussed without concrete, clearly defined offers," he adds.

However, the foreign companies did not know the local regulations and did not know how to implement what they do elsewhere, in Serbia. "As local authorities can't issue concessions without government approval, at first they thought about a public-private partnership, PPP, . . . as an easier option," he said.

"But since a company, owned by the municipalities had already been formed, involvement of a private partner would have required the changing of the statute of the company, and would have needed the approval of all of the assemblies of the founding municipalities," Sredojevic said.

Exactly why the partnership had failed, Sredojevic declined to specify, noting that power in the local authorities have changed in the meantime. The chair of the board of directors of Duboko, Petar Domanovic, from Cacak, confirmed that the offers from foreign companies had not been concrete or clearly defined. Another obstacle had been the question of prices, he added.

"As an economist, I believe it was foolish not to try to find finance in other ways, when both the [Serbian] state and Europe were prepared to aid all such projects in the field of ecology," [said] Domanovic. . . .

Duboko eventually obtained funds from the European Bank for Reconstruction and Development, EBRD. The €5 million loan [approximately $6.7 million] was the first loan from the EBRD to have been given to a Serbian municipality without guarantees from the state.

Additionally, the European Commission donated €3.8 million [approximately $5.2 million] and the Serbian government, through the Fund for Environmental Protection and the National Investment Plan, also donated funds to the project. Further funding came from the local municipalities themselves. According to the director of the company, Ivan Djokic, some 60 per cent of the work has been finished to date.

Chronic Waste Problems Outside of Major Cities

Vranje, the main regional centre in the south of Serbia, decided to solve its waste problem with its own money. In 2002, it was the first municipality in Serbia, using its own resources, to build a landfill according to European ecological standards.

This served the town alone. In late 2009, a protocol was signed envisaging the expansion of the Meteris landfill into a regional landfill serving Surdulica, Vladicin Han, Trgoviste, Bujanovac and Presevo as well.

Southern Serbia has a chronic problem with waste, which is most visible in the poor municipalities of Vladicin Han and Trgoviste. In Vladicin Han, which has no legal landfill, infectious diseases appeared last year [2009] due to irregular waste disposal.

Although the Ministry of Environment [and Spatial Planning], through the Fund for Environmental Protection, can assist with creation of regional landfills, these underdeveloped municipalities have obvious problems in meeting their part of the deal.

Fazila Azemovic, head of local economic development in Bujanovac, . . . [mentioned] that their town was working on

63

constructing a transfer station where waste would be selected and prepared for sending to Meteris.

"It is hard, because this year we were denied [a] lot of money . . . from the Republic [i.e., the government], and from the Coordination Body [the government board for the border region]. However, although it is unpopular to talk about deadlines, I expect Bujanovac to finish its part of the job by the end of 2010," she said.

This municipality obtained significant funding to draft project documentation from the Fund for Environmental Protection. The town hopes to get the remaining money it needs from the European Commission, "which is organising a tender for ecological projects in March 2010", [said] Azemovic. . . .

Although recycling and processing communal waste is highly profitable in many developed countries, the idea has barely caught on in Serbia.

Sparsely populated areas are also having a difficult time. Such is the case in the Timocka Krajina of eastern Serbia. Big distances between towns, weak infrastructure and bad telecommunications are some reasons why foreign partners have shown little interest in their waste. Local authorities are not efficient either. The mayors of eight municipalities signed a plan for a landfill at Halovo two years ago, but nothing has moved since then.

Sasa Galic, from the Regional Agency for Development of Eastern Serbia, RARIS, says it has still not been agreed who will manage the regional landfill, or whether a landfill alone will be built or a recycling centre too. Many municipalities in the region are not clear which regional landfill they would join.

New Habits Must Be Acquired

Although recycling and processing communal waste is highly profitable in many developed countries, the idea has barely caught on in Serbia. "There is no money in Serbia in waste," says Ljubomir Niksic of A.S.A. "Waste management is a completely new field in Serbia."

Minister Dulic does not want to estimate the potential value of the market in Serbia. "At this point the situation is unclear, but waste management and recycling, renewable energy sources, ecological materials and green construction will all bring significant growth in investments, profits and new jobs," he said. The drafting of a financial plan was under way as an integral part of the National Strategy for Waste Management, he indicated.

"With the implementation of the strategy, new jobs will open up, contributing to the reduction in poverty, a greener economy and the integration into society of Roma population [Romani people from central and eastern Europe], who are currently informally involved in the collection and recycling of second waste."

In a country where bins for unwanted plastic, metal and paper are still rarely seen, it may well take time before people get used to new habits of behaviour.

Meanwhile, what is also needed is the creation of a new atmosphere. Each individual in Serbia has to start to act more responsibly towards the environment. In a country where bins for unwanted plastic, metal and paper are still rarely seen, it may well take time before people get used to new habits of behaviour.

Bangladesh's Capital Is Swimming in Waste

Dhaka Courier

In Bangladesh, waste pickers provide an invaluable service to communities; but waste picking is a thankless and hazardous job. According to the following viewpoint—taken from the Dhaka Courier, *an English-language Bangladeshi publication—children who are waste pickers are often shunned from other children, and they usually drop out of school. For both children and adults, the hazardous materials waste pickers collect and clean—including bloody hospital items and household toilet waste—cause illnesses and infections. No legal or social move has been made to protect waste pickers in Bangladesh, even though their work contributes to the country's cleanliness and economy.*

As you read, consider the following questions:

1. Why has some attention been paid to waste management in Bangladesh?
2. What are some of the hazards associated with collecting hospital waste?
3. For what are some of Bangladesh's recyclable waste materials used?

A ccording to the Solid Waste Management division of Dhaka City Corporation (DCC), 3000 to 4000 tons of waste is generated every day in the city [of Bangladesh]. In

Dhaka Courier, "Wasting Away on Waste," December 17, 2009. Reproduced by permission.

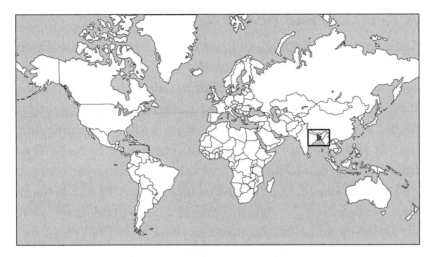

this, 50 tons is hospital waste, one-fifth of which is hazardous to health. About half the total waste is collected and dumped for landfills and the rest is scattered and left unattended all over the city. About 80% of the garbage is food waste, the rest is metal, glass, paper, polyethylene bags, cloth, etc. In total about 400,000 people are involved in clearing away the waste materials in the whole country. Dhaka City Corporation engages around 7,500 cleaners for sweeping and collecting these waste materials. There are however many more waste pickers who are not listed with the city corporation.

For disposal of these waste materials there are 2,000 dustbins and two big dumping sites in Dhaka, one at Matuail at Jatrabari and another at Boliarpur in Savar. NGOs [nongovernmental organizations] like Waste Concern, Prodipon and Prism work for solid and medical waste management in Bangladesh. Trash can generate cash; so some attention, though still inadequate, is now directed into it. But unfortunately, waste pickers do not draw as much interest as the waste. Waste picking children in Dhaka are popularly known as 'tokai', who became pathokoli (street flowers) in the words of a former president in Bangladesh. By whatever name we call them, life as a waste picker is very, very miserable.

A Thankless and Dangerous Job

These people collect reusable items from roadsides, dustbins and dumping sites, sort out the things, clean these by washing with water and sell these to waste traders. Of these people, 95% are illiterate and live below poverty line. The main income source of these families is waste picking. Men, women and children all work in this, some from dawn to dusk. They handle materials hazardous to health and have their hands and legs scratched and cut several times a day by sharp materials while sifting through the garbage. Household toilet waste and hospital waste pose a great risk of infection with skin disease, diarrhoea, chronic dysentery, viral hepatitis, etc. Even NGOs who employ them in collecting, sorting and washing hospital waste like blood bags, dressing materials, needles, syringes, etc., do not provide them with any protective measures like masks or gloves. These waste pickers who handle medical waste are especially vulnerable to infection with severe diseases.

In this course of recycling, the only thing that remains constant is the life of a waste picker, who lives as miserable a life as before.

One scavenger can earn around Tk. 100 [100 taka, or approximately $1.45] in a day. It is hard for them to go to school by leaving the chance of earning this money from scavenging. In case of their enrollment in school, they find it difficult to mix with their classmates because other learners hesitate to accept them as close friends because of the differences in their social positions. As a result, it is more likely for them to be dropping out eventually. The commitment of the government of bringing all children in school by 2011 is very likely to fail without any specific plans addressing the needs of these and other likewise hard-to-reach children in the country.

Waste picking is not as much a free occupation as it might sound. Waste traders give them loans with the commitment that they would sell the items they pick up to those particular traders only for about half the actual market price. Some dumping sites are also given on lease to waste traders. Waste pickers are forced to sell their items found in these sites at less than market rate to these traders. Any valuable items found there by waste pickers go into the hands of these traders.

Waste pickers make a large contribution to the cleanliness of our environment as well as economic development. About 87,000 people are involved in collecting recyclable waste materials in Dhaka. Plastic industries in Dhaka make shoes, buckets, toys, etc., from waste plastic materials. There are more than 200 factories for grinding the left-out plastic bottles and later exporting the material to China and Thailand, which is then turned into nylon thread and fabrics. Making cash out of trash is a thriving business in Bangladesh and can gain even more potential in the coming days with foreign investors showing their increasing interest in the sector.

In this course of recycling, the only thing that remains constant is the life of a waste picker, who lives as miserable a life as before, without access to adequate food, safe drinking water, sanitation, decent living room, education, health facilities, and all the other human rights issues everyone is so fond of preaching continuously in this country. No one has yet taken any promising initiative for improving the conditions of their lives; no legal measure has been put in place yet for the protection of their fundamental rights in a practical manner.

In Mexico City, Soon There Will Be No Place to Put Trash

Diego Cevallos

In the following viewpoint, Diego Cevallos, a Mexico-based journalist for Inter Press Service (IPS), warns that soon there will be no place to put Mexico City's ever-mounting garbage. The city's Bordo Poniente dump, which has long been overflowing, emits 2 million tons of carbon-based gases into the atmosphere each year. While closing the dump would help ease this part of the environmental dilemma, Cevallos notes that without it, there will be no place for Mexico City to put its garbage. Worse yet, the dump is only the beginning of Mexico City's environmental problems.

As you read, consider the following questions:

1. What are the two main sources of greenhouse gases in Mexico City?
2. What percentage of Mexico City's population separates its garbage for recycling?
3. Why did Mexico City's environmental secretary want to postpone shutting down Bordo Poniente?

If the municipal government of Mexico City were to keep its promises, laid out in laws and plans from 2003 and 2004, the treatment of the 12,300 tons of garbage produced daily by

Diego Cevallos, "Time Running Out for Mexico City's Garbage," *Tierramérica*, September 15, 2008. Reproduced by permission.

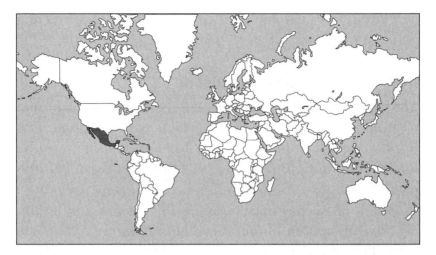

the metropolis would be more environmentally friendly. But instead there is a threat of collapse and a huge contaminated area.

The Bordo Poniente dump emits two million tons of carbon-based gases into the atmosphere each year, which represents 15 percent of the greenhouse effect gases produced by this city of nine million people, second only to automobiles, the main source of climate changing gases. Closing down the dump would be the equivalent of taking some 500,000 cars off the roads. After at least four postponements in five years, the Bordo Poniente, opened in 1985 in the east of the capital, will be shut down in January. [As of February 2010, the dump remained open.] But for now there is no alternative dump site, although the authorities are considering various possibilities.

"The situation is complicated and time is running out, but the authorities are making an effort and we are confident that a crisis will not erupt," said Alfonso De la Torre, an expert in municipal waste management and head of the environmental management department at the Autonomous Metropolitan University.

"The citizens have no idea what they might face if there is no place to put the garbage," [said] De la Torre. . . .

Mexico City's Dump Problem

The city lacks money to close down the dump in compliance with environmental standards, which require engineering works and possibly the construction of a gas emissions collector to generate electricity. The cost would be about 100 million dollars.

Nearly all of the capital's waste management plans, including the construction of four recycling and energy centers and a new fleet of garbage trucks, fail to make it from paper to reality or lag far behind schedule.

The 2004 Integrated Program for Solid Waste Management, which called for setting up the recycling and energy centers and closing down the Bordo dump, projected that by 2008 three-quarters of the residents of Mexico City should be separating household waste for recycling. [As of 2009], less than 10 percent of the people in the capital do so.

Official studies indicate there are another 130 unauthorized garbage dumps in ravines, green areas and vacant lots around the city, and some 6,000 in the areas surrounding the capital. The dumps foment harmful fauna, like rats, and the liquid runoff from the decomposing waste filters into water supplies.

> *"The authorities must see this moment of shutting down Bordo Poniente as an opportunity to move from pragmatism to a new framework for waste management, because the current model no longer works."*

De la Torre admits that there are no studies about the real impact of the illegal dumps on the environment, but he believes the effects remain limited. However, the president of the

Mexican Federation of Sanitary Engineering, Jorge Sánchez, believes that "the capital has hit bottom."

"The authorities must see this moment of shutting down Bordo Poniente as an opportunity to move from pragmatism to a new framework for waste management, because the current model no longer works," [said] Sánchez. . . .

The government, which owns the Bordo Poniente land, ordered its permanent closure when it realized it was saturated and threatens to contaminate the aquifer and water channels. The municipality asked for more time, but finally agreed to shut it down.

The 375-hectare dump has been receiving the bulk of the capital's waste since the 1980s. Ninety percent of the more than 12,000 tons of garbage arriving daily—half of it domestic—is buried, the rest is sold and recycled.

Resistance to Change

If the plans made more than four years ago by the capital's government—led since 1997 by the left-leaning Democratic Revolutionary Party (PRD)—had been carried out, by now the city would be well on its way towards sustainable management of its waste.

The goals, now redefined, were to recycle 20 percent of the waste, use 45 percent for energy generation, set aside 20 percent to produce fertilizer and bury the remaining 15 percent. With the closure of the Bordo Poniente dump, the municipality is negotiating with the neighboring state governments the possibility of sending them the garbage for a set amount of time and promising to have at least one of the recycling and energy centers up and running in 20 months.

"There is no other alternative than to make a leap in waste management, so we are hoping that the plans come in with funding, clear timelines and programs aimed at involving the citizens, which is fundamental," said the president of the Mexican Federation of Sanitary Engineering.

Mexico's Environmental Numbers

According to the Associated Press, "Mexico City wants to turn one of the planet's biggest and messiest waste management systems into the greenest in Latin America, if not the developing world."

• 2,800 environmental services companies operate in Mexico.

• 92,000 tons of solid waste is generated in Mexico every day.

• 80% of generated waste is collected in Mexico. Only 50% of this amount receives proper handling, confinement or treatment.

Waste & Recycling Expo Mexico,
"Waste and Recycling Expo Mexico:
International Trade Show for Waste Management,
Collection and Recycling Technologies,"
www.wasterecyclingmexico.com.

Martha Delgado, environmental secretary of the capital's government, says it would have been better to postpone the Bordo Poniente closure, because "the new waste management model is a matter that will take several years" to resolve. In September 2007, Delgado admitted that despite the 2003 solid waste law, which has yet to be enacted, and the 2004 management plan, the capital had been "incapable" of coming up with a new way to handle its garbage.

In late August [2009], the authorities announced bidding for the work needed to close down the Bordo Poniente dump and the construction of the energy and recycling centers, with the aim of sharing the costs with the private sector.

Meanwhile, the vast majority of the residents continue to set out their garbage without separating the different materials—and nearly all of it ends up in Bordo Poniente. Some 2,500 trucks carry the garbage. Half of the vehicles are more than 10 years old and some have been around since 1965. The trucks themselves pollute, and they lack space to carry separated materials.

"There is no long-term vision, but this cannot continue, because soon there will be no place to put the garbage."

The city now has 250 modern garbage trucks, but needs more than 2,000. The city officials recognize that such a purchase is beyond the means of the municipal budget.

University expert De la Torre attributes the lack of action by the authorities to "society's resistance to change," political problems and lack of resources. However, sanitation engineering president Sánchez believes the problem lies in the short-term culture of the government leaders and their reticence to upset the voters. "There is no long-term vision, but this cannot continue, because soon there will be no place to put the garbage," he said.

Periodical Bibliography

The following articles have been selected to supplement the diverse views presented in this chapter.

AllAfrica.com	"Tanzania: Zanzibar's Sewage Disposal Challenge," April 23, 2010. http://allafrica.com.
Roger Boyes	"Welcome Aboard the Garbage Express from Italy to Germany," *Times* (London), June 13, 2008.
Lisa Kaas Boyle	"Recycling Plastic: What a Waste," *Huffington Post*, September 16, 2009.
Ed Cumming	"The Biggest Dump in the World," *Telegraph* (UK), March 16, 2010.
European Environment Agency	"How Can Waste Policy Contribute to a Resource-Efficient Economy?" April 20, 2010. www.eea.europa.eu.
Jane Fynes-Clinton	"The Garbage Generation," *Courier-Mail* (Queensland, Australia), January 20, 2010.
Elizabeth Grossman	"Where Computers Go to Die—and Kill," *Salon*, April 10, 2006.
Mike Melia	"A Second Garbage Patch: Plastic Seen in Atlantic," *USA Today*, April 16, 2010.
Gillian Murdoch	"Trash and Burn: Singapore's Waste Problem," Reuters, May 22, 2008.
Wallace J. Nichols	"Our Plastic Ocean Turns Forty," *Huffington Post*, April 21, 2010.
Lisa Acho Remorenko	"Keep Our Oceans Clean: For the Sake of Marine Life, Throw Trash Away," *Santa Barbara Independent*, April 23, 2010.
Alessio Vinci	"Why Naples Is Drowning in Garbage," CNN, January 8, 2008.

CHAPTER 2

The Controversial Nature of Garbage and Recycling

In the United Kingdom and Around the World, People Debate the Value of Recycling

Leo Hickman

Leo Hickman is a features journalist and editor at the Guardian, *a daily newspaper in the United Kingdom. In this viewpoint, he provides in-depth information about waste disposal. According to Hickman, many people simply recycle and feel good about it, without finding out the important details. For one, recyclable materials are a commodity and therefore suffer through the ups and downs of the marketplace. Other details, which must be considered by city officials, involve choices about using landfills and incinerators, and recycling locally instead of abroad.*

As you read, consider the following questions:

1. According to Ian Wakelin, why will "co-mingled" recycling improve the perception the public has of recycling?
2. In descending order, what is the "waste hierarchy," according to the waste industry, and why is it important for people to know it?
3. According to Paul Andrews, in what ways are modern-day incinerators superior to older ones?

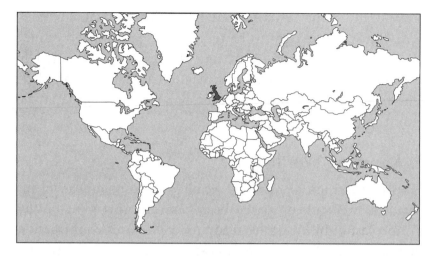

Several times a year, without forewarning or invitation, inspectors representing the Chinese government make their way to the Black Country, the geographical and, some would argue, industrial heart of England, to rummage through the recycling collected from the region's streets. They pass through Walsall and on to neighbouring Aldridge where they visit a former foundry that was recently converted—"recycled", according to its owners—into the country's largest "materials recovery facility" (MRF, pronounced "merf").

"We had them here again just a few weeks ago," says Mick Davis, the business development director at Greenstar, the site's owners. From a gantry high up above the loud confusion of conveyor belts, thrashing bag splitters and giant spinning magnets below, he points to a towering pile of bales being stacked by a forklift truck in the corner of the hangar-like building. The sweet, acidic stench of rotting refuse attacks the nostrils.

"The inspectors reserve the right to split open any of those bales containing plastic bottles and check for quality and contamination," says Davis. "They are very fussy about standards. They will also closely inspect our 'soft mix' paper bales, too. We now have to take a photograph of every bale before it gets shipped to China. It's all about traceability and quality control. But it's their right to be fussy: They pay us good money for these materials. We're getting about £50 [approximately $75.00] for a 300 kg [approximately 661 lbs.] PET [polyethylene terephthalate, a thermoplastic polymer resin] bale at the moment."

Is Recycling Worthwhile?

This is the vision of recycling we all want to hold dear in our heads as we wash up baked bean cans and sort wine bottles from plastic milk cartons ready for collection: confirmation that as much of our waste as possible is collected, sorted and sold on for a profit.

But the reality—somewhat at odds with the evidence to be found in Aldridge—is that recycling is undergoing a crisis of confidence. Amid stories of old televisions being sent for recycling but instead heading for Nigerian landfill sites, and popular revolts against "bin taxes" and fortnightly collections, many householders say they are beginning to lose confidence in a system that has only been in existence for the last decade. (It's easy to forget that as recently as 2000, as much as 90% of waste in England was still being sent to landfill: In 2008, it stood at 59.9% of household waste.) Compounding this sense of anxiety is the news that the international market for recyclable commodities has taken a dive alongside the rest of the global economy, sparking headlines about piles of unsold recycled materials across the country.

And hovering over this are longer-term questions about the direction our waste management strategy is headed, with an increasing push towards incineration as landfill is slowly squeezed out of the equation by ever-tightening environmental directives, regulations and taxes. Would it, in fact, make more sense both environmentally and economically, as one government waste adviser controversially suggested recently, to be burning some of our recycling to generate both electricity and heat instead of, say, exporting it?

Inside the warmth of the boardroom, away from the noise and hurry of the machinery, Ian Wakelin, Greenstar's CEO, offers up a passionate defence of recycling: "Yes, there is a backlash against recycling at the moment, but there is also a real lack of balance in the debate. Is recycling being landfilled, as some are claiming? Beyond the contaminated matter that we have to extract from the recyclate we receive [about 5–10% of the total weight], I think this is nonsense. I haven't talked to anyone in the recycling industry who has landfilled anything that is recyclable. The economics just don't stack up. Why would they when landfill gate fees are so high? [Currently, the fee is about £50–60 (approximately $75 to $90) a tonne.] They can give it to me and I will readily take it off them."

Making Recycling Easier

Wakelin feels that the UK [United Kingdom] still has a long way to go before it feels at ease about how it deals with its waste. "We are such a nimby culture here in the UK," he says. "Would you rather have a landfill or an incinerator on your doorstep? Look at Vienna [Austria], where they've built an incinerator right in the centre of the city that is so beautiful that it now attracts tourists. The danger is that public perception is bloody difficult to change. We need more positive education programmes about what we do with our waste. For example, it's immoral not to ship our recycling back to India and China if it's helping them to grow their economies and develop. Who are we to deny them this resource?"

Wakelin believes that one of the tricks to winning over a skeptical public is to make recycling far easier for the average householder. "I always get asked the same questions at dinner parties," he says. "Why do I have to have so many bins at home? And why can't I recycle more plastic?"

The solution, says Wakelin, is to "leave it to the machines", rather than have "Mr and Mrs Average sorting it all at home". His company's philosophy for waste is that "co-mingled" collections (where all dry recyclables are placed by householders into just one bag ready for collection) are the way forward, as opposed to kerbside [curbside] collections (where householders are expected to separate their recycling at home for refuse workers working "kerbside" to then put these sorted materials by hand into separate containers on their vehicle) which, he says, are less efficient, both environmentally and economically. The MRF at Aldridge processes 500–600 tonnes of municipal recycling (collected from households, restaurants, small businesses etc.) a day, serving 15 local authorities, some as far away as London and North Wales. This represents 3–4% of the UK's dry recyclate.

"The traditional argument against co-mingled is that it gets more contaminated than kerbside," he says. "That was the case five to 10 years ago, but the technology is much better now. The industry is going through a revolution right now, from the rag-and-bone man through to the machine. We are seeing a rush by councils towards co-mingling. Nine out of the 10 best-performing local authorities, when it comes to recycling rates, use co-mingled collections. When they switch over, they typically see a 20% leap in recycling rates overnight."

Recycling Locally

Back out on the shop floor, Davis edges past the 40-strong team of "pickers", who are all intently scanning the recycling as it flashes past them on the conveyor for any contamination missed by the machines. "We see all this as a commodity, not waste," he says. "We then process it into soft-mix paper, glass, aluminum, metal cans and soft plastics by polymer type and colour. About 10–15% of our materials go to China, but the majority stays in the UK. All our newsprint, for example, goes to a processing site in Aylesbury.

"Steel cans used to go to the steel firm Corus, but they have currently abandoned this due to the downturn in the car industry. Last year we were getting £60 [approximately $90] a tonne for steel, but that's down to £30–£50 [approximately $45 to $75]. Yes, this has hurt us. But we are tied to the global economy and we think the sharpest shocks are over. People had been running down their stocks of recycled materials, especially in China, but now that they've exhausted those supplies they are coming back into the market and prices have strengthened again. It's a total myth that we can't sell this stuff. The main problem is that there's a real shortage of processing facilities like this around the country."

Chris Allen is one of the reprocessors waiting keenly "downstream" for these materials to turn them back into "useful stuff". As CEO of Smurfit Kappa Paper UK, he oversees a firm that produces 450,000 tonnes of 100% recycled brown paper at two paper mills, in Kent and Birmingham, for use by corrugated box manufacturers across the UK and Ireland. "We turn things such as newspaper, old cardboard boxes and cornflake packets into quality brown paper," he says. "The UK produces 2m [million] tonnes of cardboard boxes a year. We should do our level best to produce these with locally recycled materials. At the moment, I'm paying £50–55 [approximately $75 to $82] a tonne for mixed waste paper and card, whereas I'm selling it as brown paper for £280 [approximately $419] a tonne. This is a viable business, believe me. The fibres from those trees that get cut down have a bloody good life."

The Market Is Recovering, but Is the Quality Good?

Allen has strong views about media reports that some local authorities and collection companies have been stockpiling paper, and other sorts of recycling, as market prices have collapsed: "The Chinese buy paper in huge volume and have been outbidding us. They had been buying like hell and paying incredible sums for it. But the downturn caught up with China at the end of last year and they suddenly stopped buying the expensive stuff from far-off Europe. But they are now coming back into the market and we are seeing prices rise again. There's always been ups and downs in the market, but it was the collection companies who had been exclusively selling to the Chinese that were bleating at the end of last year that the market had collapsed. I hate to say, 'I told you so,' but if they had had a balanced supply portfolio they wouldn't have been in that pickle. The quiet, sensible ones just got on with selling to buyers like me. Look at Birmingham City Council, the largest local authority in the country. They didn't have one single problem, because they sell paper that is well sorted and of a high quality. It's the shit-quality paper that you saw being stockpiled on the TV."

Tom Freyberg, editor of *Recycling & Waste World* magazine, agrees there are signs the market is recovering from its trough in December 2008. "Problems started in October when the prices of materials such as paper and plastics fell dramatically," he says. "However, prices are now climbing. For people to lose faith now in recycling would be disastrous."

But it's not just the availability of buyers that has helped to depress prices, say some prominent voices within the industry. There is a problem with quality, too. The Campaign for Real Recycling, which is made up of some of the UK's largest materials reprocessors, in addition to community recycling representatives and Friends of the Earth, argues that the overall quality of recycled materials in the UK just isn't as high as it should and could be, and that this is largely down to the trend for co-mingled collections.

Earlier this year, the campaign group sent an open letter to Jane Kennedy MP [member of Parliament], the minister for farming and environment at Defra [Department for Environment, Food and Rural Affairs], urging the government to reverse this trend. It lamented the fact that the recycling system in the UK was producing "extremely low-grade mixed materials masquerading as paper, aluminum, glass" and, as a result, many reprocessors were having to import materials from abroad unnecessarily.

"For people to lose faith now in recycling would be disastrous."

Engaging the Public

Caught in the middle of this debate is the Waste and Resources Action Programme (Wrap), the not-for-profit company set up as part of the government's waste strategy published back in 2000. Phillip Ward, as director for local government services, has the task of advising local authorities on what types of collection systems they should opt for.

"We are going through a large transitionary period," he says. "As recently as 2000 we were largely putting all our stuff in the ground. But we're now at 35% recycling rates. Local authorities had to invent a new system but no one knew the best way to do it. That's why we now have a patchwork solution across the country. It's not a finished system yet."

Yes, he says, we must all aim to produce cleaner, better quality recyclate, as well as aim to "narrow the variations between the local authorities", but he adds that a patchwork of collection and sorting methods will always be necessary to some degree due to the rural/suburban/urban split across the country. Co-mingling better suits the often cramped "internal logistics" of people living in built-up city centres, whereas kerbside collection suits those out in the leafy suburbs with enough space to sort everything into neat, tidy piles.

Psychology plays an important role in public engagement, says Ward. "Surveys have shown that most people have fairly mundane criticisms of recycling: 'Nobody explains to me what happens next to my waste', or 'Nobody says thank you for my efforts'. People do respond to this, rather than a punitive atmosphere."

Tackling Waste Reduction

Ward accepts that the media backlash ("propaganda by papers with an agenda," as he describes it) against "pay-as-you-throw" schemes, which aimed to impose an extra charge on householders who produced excessive waste, means that these are now politically untenable. Give people the right signals, as well as the right collections, he says, and most people are only too happy to "do their bit". "Our research has shown that giving people two 55-litre [approximately 14 gallons] boxes for recycling, collected once a week, is the ideal combination. We have also found that if you get plastic recycling right it triggers further engagement. This is now a key area for us, alongside increasing food waste collections. [According to Wrap, we still throw out about one-third of the food we buy.] The next frontier is getting plastic items such as yoghurt pots and margarine lids collected. It has to be shown to be viable. For example, a new plant called Closed Loop has recently opened in Dagenham, Essex, processing plastic milk cartons and clear drinks bottles into food-grade packaging."

We need a manufacturing system that uses far more recycled materials.

But Ward also wants us all to ask some broader, deeper questions about our whole "cradle-to-grave" waste economy. The waste industry has been talking about the so-called "waste hierarchy" for decades—the mantra that places waste prevention as the first goal followed, in descending order, by minimisation, reuse, recycling, energy recovery and, finally, disposal—but it has still not yet fully met these words with deeds. After all, it is now almost 50 years since the US [United States] social critic Vance Packard wrote about the excessive waste produced by Western consumerism (principally, how we are all encouraged to buy things we don't need) in his landmark best seller *The Waste Makers*—the *Silent Spring* of the waste world—and still we have yet to fundamentally heed his warnings.

"We need a manufacturing system that uses far more recycled materials," says Ward. "We need to tackle planned obsolescence [when a product becomes non-functional after a certain period in a way that was planned by the manufacturer; it benefits the manufacturer because it requires the consumer to purchase again]. At the moment it's still hard to make the economic case to mend something, but, as we have already seen in places such as Japan and Taiwan, the labour pool in China will become less and less cheap as their standard of living rises. This should lead to the return of the repairman for items such as broken dishwashers, kettles and washing machines. We can do this by getting the manufacturers together. That's how we tackled standby power. Ten years ago, standby used 25–30 watts; now that's down to 1–2 watts."

Incinerators Are Inevitable

Ask most householders what their No. 1 irritant is when it comes to waste and the response is immediate: excessive packaging. Why is the onus placed on householders and consumers to dispose of it dutifully and correctly, they ask, when the problem could be more readily tackled upstream? The Local Government Authority also recently weighed into the debate saying that supermarkets should contribute towards the costs of recycling, adding that almost 40% of the packaging used by supermarkets still cannot be easily recycled.

Ward shares this frustration, but he doesn't have a word of comfort for those who express concern about the slow creep towards incineration as opposed to, say, waste minimisation or greatly increased recycling. "Incineration is going to be inevitable," says Ward. "[But the] cleaner we can get our waste, the less of it we'll need to burn. That's why we always plead for people to keep their recycling as clean and well sorted as possible. Curry sauce all over your recycling will render it useless."

There are those, though, who believe that recovering energy by incinerating waste is better, by and large, than recycling it. The Institute of Mechanical Engineers, for example, has recently urged the government to invest in heating and energy projects with local waste being used as the fuel resource, much like the schemes found in countries such as Germany and Austria. "The government should abandon its focus on recycling as the only way to rid us of landfills," it says, "as this is quite unachievable and is clearly deceiving the public about what is really happening to their waste. Recycling should only be for waste products that cannot be more sustainably converted into electricity, heat and/or transport fuels."

"Incineration is going to be inevitable . . . but the cleaner we get our waste, the less of it we'll need to burn."

Combined Methods of Waste Management

Adam Read, a former professor of waste management at Northampton University, believes that the industry is still in the foothills when it comes to understanding the full environmental implications of each form of waste treatment. "We certainly need to understand our waste flow better," he says. "We need a better grasp of the calorific values, water content, market values and the like of each waste source before pushing ahead. Yes, it sometimes will be more economical to burn waste, but the environmental impact is always going to be less when recycling. However, incineration will always be better environmentally than landfill because of the methane generated when organic waste rots underground."

On the site of a former quarry at Allington in Kent sits a facility that is squarely at the heart of the debate about whether we should be burning more of our waste, especially the portions of our waste that some argue could and should be recovered for recycling. The Enviropower energy from waste (EFW) facility, with its 80m-tall [approximately 262 feet] chimney, is the country's newest and largest incinerator. It also operates a MRF and, as a result, can now claim to be Kent's one-stop-shop for waste. The Waste Recycling Group, the Spanish-owned company that built the site, says the UK can expect to see more and more combined "waste management facilities" such as Allington quarry being built in the coming years.

"We burn 1,500 tonnes of waste a day—24/7, 365 days a year—at temperatures of 600–650C [degrees Celsius]," says Paul Andrews, Enviropower's managing director, as a huge mechanical claw swoops down, grabs several tonnes of black bin bags from a concrete bunker below, and lifts them up into a shredder in preparation for entering the combustion chambers. "Doing so provides us with 43 megawatts of electricity—easily enough to power the whole of Maidstone."

Easing Incinerator Concerns

As much of the recyclable material as possible, he explains, is recovered from the black bins as they pass through the shredders, but this only amounts realistically to any ferrous metals that manage to be caught by magnets. The vast majority of what Kent now puts into its black bin bags—chicken bones, bottle tops, cling film, nappies—ends up being burned inside Allington quarry's fluidised-bed combustion chambers (ovens with 120 tonnes of sand at the bottom that is blasted with air to help increase the "burn efficiency" of the materials that pass over it). It's a one-way ticket, but Enviropower says by burning this waste it helps to divert almost half a million tonnes of Kent's waste from going to landfill each year. For every black bag that passes into the system, 85% of the weight will be vapourised and the remaining 15% will be extracted, either as an anaerobic sludge or a dry ash. The sludge is sent to landfill, whereas the ash is either landfilled or used as aggregate for roads.

"Zero waste is just not possible. We live in a society where some waste streams just don't have a home other than disposal."

But what most of the surrounding residents want to know is what is coming out of that tall chimney. When the site was going through planning, for example, local campaigners opposing its construction said they were fearful of being exposed to soot, heavy metals, PCBs (polychlorinated biphenyl) and cancerous dioxins. Paul Andrews makes a pretty remarkable defence when probed on this matter: "It would take 25 years for this facility to produce as much pollution as is emitted by vehicles on the M25 [a major motorway/highway in the UK; the longest city bypass in the world] in just three days. The legal limit for dust particles from a coal-fired power station is 160mg per cubic metre, whereas for us the limit is 10mg per cubic metre. Proportionally, fireworks throw up far more in the way of dioxins; so does cooking bacon. We have even reached the limit of detection with some of the gases, but we could still go further with nitrogen oxides. The regulations on emissions are incredibly stringent now and, to be honest, we would welcome even tighter rules."

Andrews says that when most people think of incinerators now they think of the ones dating back to the postwar period. But today's incinerators, he says, are many orders of magnitude cleaner because they go to "extraordinary lengths" to clean up the gases as they leave the combustion chamber, including passing them through a lime and carbon bath to remove the acidic gases and through filter bags to remove dust particles.

Laying Out a Clear Waste Vision

"We have this Englishman-and-his-castle attitude here in the UK," he says. "Zero waste is just not possible. We live in a society where some waste streams just don't have a home other than disposal. As a country, we need to work out where we are ultimately heading with waste. The government needs to set out clearly what our waste vision is."

Recycling as much of our waste as possible is still the goal, says Andrews, but we must accept that some of it will need to be either incinerated or landfilled. But the wider, as yet unanswered, question is what happens when incinerating waste is seen to be more convenient than going to the cost and bother of recycling it? Do we block this from happening with regulation and taxes, as we are doing with landfill, or do we slide into a society that predominately incinerates its waste? The way Liz Parkes, head of waste at the Environment Agency, sees it, we are going through some inevitable growing pains as we move from a nation that once unthinkingly threw its waste in the ground and buried it to one that attempts to make as much use of it as it can.

"Recycling has to be normalised and socially acceptable. Just look at what happened with issues such as smoking and drink-driving over the years."

"Yes, it is taking time to turn this around, and it's a shame that the current debate could turn attitudes away from recycling, but there is a demand out there for our materials," she says. "We have to keep building up public trust with things such as open days and school visits. We must keep the message simple. Recycling has to be normalised and socially acceptable. Just look at what happened with issues such as smoking and drink-driving [driving a vehicle while under the influence of alcohol] over the years. It takes time as this is really all about public behaviour. We just need to move as a society from one that says 'not there, not there' to one that asks, 'Where do you want it then?'"

In Canada, Calgary's Curbside Recycling Sparks Concerns About Recycling

Kevin Libin

In 2009 Calgary became Canada's last major city to adopt a curbside recycling program; the program represented the city's ultimate goal to recycle 80 percent of its residents' trash. While many lauded the program, some believe it is misdirected, according to Kevin Libin, a journalist for the National Post. *In this viewpoint, Libin makes the argument that too much recycling can be as bad, or worse, for communities and the environment than no recycling at all. Libin agrees with experts who claim that no city should aim for more than a 35 percent recycling rate of trash.*

As you read, consider the following questions:

1. According to J. Winston Porter, what is the only really valuable material to recycle?
2. What is a harmful environmental effect of excessive residential recycling programs?
3. According to the viewpoint, why can't incinerators usually compete with landfills?

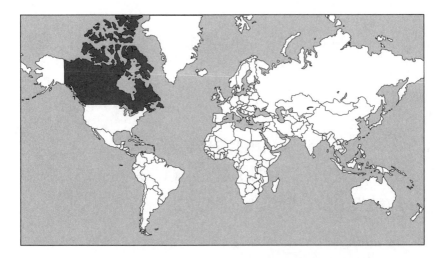

The City of Calgary introduced its blue box, curbside recycling program this year [2009], and there was rejoicing.
Calgary, the last major Canadian city to offer it, had, until recently, asked citizens to deliver their own recyclables to green
bins located every few blocks, or to hire, at $10 a month, a
private pickup service. To those concerned about environmental appearances, it was embarrassing.

"It means something to me that we're the last large city in
Canada to implement curbside recycling," said Druh Farrell,
the alderman championing the program.

> *If the aim is to help the environment, Calgary, ironically,*
> *may have been just as well off in the Stone Age.*

Approving the $50-million plan (plus another roughly $50
million a year recycling tax on homeowners) meant that Calgary had emerged from the "Stone Age," sighed a columnist
with the *Calgary Herald*, relieved of being "the laughingstock
of the country" for living in a city of eco-barbarians.

If symbolism, and the urge to feel ecologically righteous,
were the objective, then the blue box program—part of the
city's ambitious goal to divert 80% of trash from landfills by

2020—succeeded the moment it began. But if the aim is to help the environment, Calgary, ironically, may have been just as well off in the Stone Age.

Metal Pays, Glass Doesn't

Before this year, Calgary was already diverting more than 20% of city waste from landfills through private arrangements. In terms of making an environmental difference, that's getting close to what cities should aim for, says J. Winston Porter, who, as former assistant administrator for America's Environmental Protection Agency, was the first to establish nationwide recycling targets in the United States in the 1980s. His target then was 25%, and it's a number he largely sticks by. Diverting 35% of waste into recycling is about as a high as any city can justify, he says.

Trying to recycle more can be wasteful, if not harmful, he says, even though many major cities are setting targets at 70% or higher.

"People say you can't recycle too much. It turns out you can," says Mr. Porter, president of the environmental consulting firm, the Waste Policy Center, near Washington, D.C. "If you spend enough money, you can recycle anything. That doesn't mean you should."

While a blue bin out front makes us feel we're helping the planet, recycling most household materials has either minimal environmental impact, or even a negative one. Homeowners dutifully put out their glass, plastic, steel and aluminum packaging. But the only really valuable item, Mr. Porter says, is the metal. That sounds like an economic assessment, but it's a key environmental measure: resources to make metal are at a premium, and production is energy intensive. Recycling metal pays because it saves on limited resources and energy—in other words, it's better for the environment. The trouble is that in the typical North American city's solid waste stream (including trash and recyclables) aluminum and steel generally account for just 2% by weight. Glass sent to recycling facilities is heavier, making up 3 to 5% of typical city waste by weight. But although it demands more energy, there isn't much use for it.

All the glass collected this year by Calgary's new program ended up at the East Calgary Landfill, where it is piling up for want of a buyer. "It's a product that there just isn't any demand for," Bill Stitt, general manager of Metro Waste Paper Recovery Inc., the city's recycling contractor, told a local paper. Edmonton is stockpiling, too, as are a number of other Canadian cities. The price of sand [the main ingredient for glass] is simply too cheap, and the impracticality of reusing bottles of varying quality and colour is too big a headache to make it marketable.

While a blue bin out front makes us feel we're helping the planet, recycling most household materials has either minimal environmental impact, or even a negative one.

Glass is a "red herring when talking about recyclables," a Recycling Council of BC [British Columbia] spokeswoman conceded to the CBC [Canadian Broadcasting Corporation] this year; since it doesn't break down, there's no effect on air or water when it's buried in landfills. A 2003 study by Enviros Consulting UK found that "from a global warming perspective, there is limited environmental benefit to using recycled glass" but continuing with the exercise of recycling was "an important part of the UK meeting its overall glass recycling targets." That is, so politicians could meet their set goals, even if there was no environmental point to it.

The Costs and Effects of Recycling

Unfortunately, recycling plastic often doesn't make much more sense. Germany has stockpiled millions of tonnes of recyclable

Knowing the Three Rs

Although recycling positively impacts the environment, it is not highest . . . on the "RRR hierarchy." According to the U.S. Environmental Protection Agency, . . . the hierarchy is as follows:

Reduce—Reduce the amount of goods you use. Ways to reduce include:

1. Buy fewer items you do not need.

2. Buy bulk items, . . . which eliminates the need for packaging.

3. Walk, bike, or carpool, which reduces the amount of oil used.

Reuse—Reuse items. Ways to reuse include:

1. Buy secondhand clothing, or organize clothing swaps. . . .

2. Repair broken or ripped items instead of replacing them.

3. Use recycled materials in artwork and household projects.

Recycle—Recycle anything that you can not reuse. If your community does not have mandatory recycling, there are still options:

1. Even if your local garbage collection company does not have curbside recycling, it might collect recyclables on site.

2. There may be private recycling companies in your town.

3. Many companies will recycle their used items returned to them by customers. . . .

U.S. Environmental Protection Agency,
"Wastes—Resource Conservations—Reduce, Reuse, Recycle,"
www.epa.gov. Complied by editor.

plastics in rural fields, like aboveground dumps. "These cheap plastic bottles, it depends on the price of oil, but the market is not worth much," says Daniel Benjamin, an economist at

South Carolina's Clemson University who studies recycling. Though it makes up roughly 5%, by weight, of a typical North American garbage stream, applications for used, mixed plastic are limited. "We're talking about a few dollars a tonne," Professor Benjamin says.

San Francisco's Department of Waste recently calculated it paid $4,000 a tonne to recycle plastic bags. Its resale price for the recycled product? $32. "Nobody wants it. There's no value. It doesn't make sense," says Joseph Gho, CEO of EPI Environmental Products Inc., a Vancouver manufacturer of biodegradable plastics. "Besides the financial, the economic cost, you've got the environmental cost" of recycling unwanted material. "The trucks running out there, burning fuel . . . you have to use energy, you've got CO_2 [carbon dioxide] emissions."

That's why curbside recycling requires, wherever it's implemented, millions of tax dollars to stay afloat: The inputs required are greater than the savings. Even in New York City, where area land is some of the most expensive on the continent, it costs $240 to deal with a ton of recyclables, compared to the $130 a ton of landfills, says Angela Logomasini, director of risk and environmental policy at Washington, D.C.'s Competitive Enterprise Institute.

Often the effects of aggressive residential recycling programs harm environmental goals. Citywide blue box programs typically mean a whole new fleet of trucks: Calgary now has 64 more diesel-burning rigs retracing the same tracks its garbage trucks did just a few days earlier, roughly doubling carbon dioxide emissions and other pollutants.

A 2000 study by the London-based environmental group Friends of the Earth found that collecting yard waste for recycling (i.e., making mulch) emitted 264 more pounds of CO_2 than burying it in a landfill. In 2002, two of Sweden's leading environmental authorities argued that recycling's benefits were usually undone by the resources required to collect and process it. The promise of environmentalists of a "flourishing re-cycling market" where reused goods would find ready buyers "was already a dream 40 years ago and is, unfortunately, still a dream," they conceded. Better, they wrote, that most materials be incinerated at waste-to-energy plants, which is easier to do, and generates electricity, offsetting the need for fossil fuels. "We believe that incineration of household waste including disposable packaging and food waste, with energy recovery, is best for the environment, economy and management of natu-ral resources," wrote Valfrid Paulsson, former head of the Swedish Environmental Protection Agency, and Sorren Norby, former president of Keep Sweden Tidy.

Arguments for Incinerators and Landfills

The approach is catching on. Britain is building 50 new waste-to-energy incinerators; Denmark's environmental protection agency recommended in a 2002 report that the country would be best to reroute parts of its recycling program to incinera-tors instead. With pollutants having been cut dramatically from the process, and a smaller CO_2 footprint for power than coal, converting waste to energy makes as much sense to Eu-ropeans as does growing grain to burn for biofuels.

"It's done in Japan, in Europe, in Russia, all over the world, and we're actually way behind on waste-to-energy in North America," says Patrick Moore, chairman of Vancouver envi-ronmental communications firm, GreenSpirit Strategies. . . . "Wherever there's diminishing returns [on recycling], that's where we should be converting waste to energy."

The idea of burying garbage in the earth instinctively turns off some people.

Here in spacious North America, incineration can't usually compete with cheap landfills. In the late-eighties, Americans panicked over landfill shortages after a media scare set off when a garbage barge, the Mobro 4000, floated for months off the U.S. East Cost seeking a ready landfill. Its owners' bad management was the real culprit, not landfill scarcity: In fact, the U.S. and Canada both have more cheap space for landfill than anyone could ever need. "The only problem is will," says Ms. Logomasini. A study out of Washington's Gonzaga University calculated that all the garbage produced by Americans over the next 1,000 years would fit into a landfill just 44 miles square and 100 feet deep—less than one-tenth of one percent of American real estate.

The idea of burying garbage in the earth instinctively turns off some people, Mr. Porter admits. But, unless we adopt European levels of incineration, landfills are the final destination for pretty well everything we produce. "Landfills are always going to be with us," Mr. Porter says. "If I leave a foam cup resting in a landfill, I don't see why that's a problem."

A certain amount of recycling will always be with us, too. It has been for ages, wherever the value of useful materials— paper, aluminum, copper, etc.—created businesses eager to reprocess the products at their own cost. For cities determined to do their part, or, likelier, looking to seize the profitable part of the recycling business, Mr. Porter argues that there are easier, more environmentally friendly options than immense, mandatory blue box programs. First, cities should drop the ridiculously high targets to recycle 70, 80 or 90% of waste. And instead, have homeowners bundle their paper, cardboard and aluminum—the worthwhile stuff—into special coloured bags alongside their regular trash pickup. Those bags can then be separated at the landfill, and the rest trashed. That would eliminate all the extra trucks, energy and cost that so many cities incur so that green-posturing politicians can delude citizens into believing they're helping the environment, when really, they could be making things worse.

In India and Japan, Perspectives on Garbage and Recycling Are Different, but There Is a Common Thread

Urvashi Butalia

In the following viewpoint, writer Urvashi Butalia discusses the problems her friend, Chihiro, is having keeping up with Japan's strict recycling laws. In her native India, Butalia witnesses a drastically different, and much more relaxed, recycling system. But while much gets "recycled" in India, there is a growing garbage problem there, too. In the end, Butalia stresses the need for all nations to face collectively the world's garbage problem. Urvashi Butalia is the director and cofounder of Kali for Women, India's first feminist publishing house.

As you read, consider the following questions:

1. In Japan, what are "corrective classes," and who must take them?
2. Why can't Chihiro put her mounting garbage out at the curb?
3. How is recycling part of India's "informal economy"?

I'm sitting in an elegant coffee bar in Tokyo talking to my friend Chihiro. It's an unlikely place to be discussing garbage but that's the subject on her mind. A professor of politi-

Urvashi Butalia, "Garbage Blues," *New Internationalist*, vol. 384, November 2005, p. 29. Copyright © 2005 New Internationalist Magazine. Reproduced by permission.

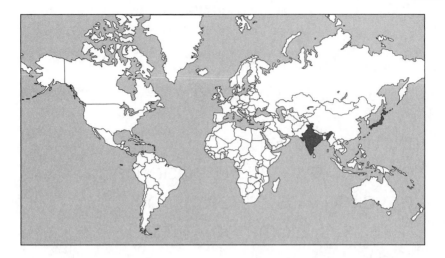

cal science at a prestigious university, Chihiro has just come back from a 'corrective class'—a couple of hours of enforced watching of videos and listening to lectures about garbage. It's her punishment for not following Japan's new rules on household waste.

It's time she can ill afford to lose. Chihiro leads a high-pressure life—lecturing at two universities, researching, publishing, organizing seminars, bringing up two young daughters, running a household. Her husband, also an academic, helps out. But even so, the burden is squarely hers.

The city of Yokohama, where Chihiro lives, has recently set up a new garbage disposal system. Homeowners are responsible for separating their garbage at source. But it's not just tin cans and paper. There's also glass and cloth and compost and, and, and ... I can't even get my head around all the categories.

Chihiro tells me she's now required to separate things according to the new categories, then deliver the packets on given days, at given times, to a central point from where they are collected. Every day of the week is marked for one kind of disposal or other. Miss a day and you have to wait a whole week. Worse, you can't really leave garbage festering outside (even if it doesn't fester, you can't leave it there; it may blow up, emit annoying smells, or just ruin the landscape . . .) and so you are obliged to keep it inside the house.

Chihiro lives in a tiny flat. There isn't room to house mountains of garbage, even if it is only a week's worth of newspapers (they get four or five a day). So, with the new rules, her house is bursting at the seams with 'stuff'. It's imperative that she get it to the collection point on time, but she's helpless. Mornings are hectic: wake the two girls, prepare their lunch, run them to school, come back, run her husband to the train station, come back, clean up, get herself together, run to the station, an hour to class . . . and so on. There isn't a morning when she can easily make it. Or, more accurately, she may just be able to make it. She doesn't really have the time to load the garbage into her car, then join the queue to unload it at the dump. But missed deadlines mean 'corrective classes'—and she shudders to think of what missed corrective classes may lead to.

We Must Face Our Garbage Problem

Chihiro finds the extra burden of managing the family garbage oppressive. She's stressed and depressed. She feels she can't cope.

Chihiro finds the extra burden of managing the family garbage oppressive. She's stressed and depressed.

I find it mystifying. This is Japan, I remind myself, one of the richest countries in the world. Is this what 'development' is all about? If so maybe we're better off in India where we don't yet have sophisticated garbage disposal rules—garbage is too valuable to waste, and recycling is part of the informal economy. Old newspapers are fashioned into paper bags, tin cans are hammered into electric stoves, plastic bottles are used

Environmental Policy in Japan

Problems associated with pollution have been documented in Japan since the nineteenth century, but economic progress and development had priority over pollution control and the protection of environmental quality. However, a series of incidents of pollution in the 1950s and 1960s led to increased public pressure on industries to act in a socially responsible manner. This spawned important legislative and regulatory measures, such as decontamination efforts, the establishment of environmental standards, and requirements for compensation for the damages caused by environmental pollution. However, this first wave of national pollution-control laws required very little of industry in contrast to international standards at the time. As a result, local citizens and regional governments placed still further pressure upon industry to strengthen pollution-control policies. A series of negotiations between local stakeholders and regional governments followed, resulting in almost every major enterprise across all sectors conceding to the demands placed upon them. These compliance arrangements, termed "Pollution Prevention Agreements," typically involved the adoption of best-available technologies.

Masayo Wakabayashi and Taisha Sugiyama,
"Japan's Keidauren Voluntary Action Plan on the Environment,"
Reality Check. Ed. Richard D. Morgenstern and William A. Pizer.
Washington, DC: RFF Press, 2007, p. 44.

to collect water or store kerosene, coconut husks scrub dishes, old rags are sewn into carrier bags. . . .

But then, I stop myself. This is not a constructive way to think. This isn't about India and Japan or the third world and first world. This is about the lives and lifestyles we are creating for ourselves and the detritus we leave behind. It's about learning to cope with the consequences of acquiring more things which are supposed to make life easier. When water started to come out of bottles rather than the tap, we were delighted because now we could carry those bottles around, until we were faced with the problem of what to do with the empties. On Indian trains they tell you to destroy the bottles, but most Indians find it difficult to destroy things that can be reused. So they leave them behind and the scavengers pick them up, fill them with ordinary water, seal them and sell them all over again. Recycling yes; but pure water, no. It's no use romanticizing ourselves just because a culture that's largely poor will find ways to reuse things.

I haven't stopped thinking of Chihiro's story since I left her. It comes back to me every day as I step out of my home and the garbage collection rickshaw comes round. I watch as two men separate plastic from paper and cardboard from tin—low castes, for who else can handle garbage in this country?

If we don't put our heads together as a society, whether in Japan or India or elsewhere, we'll end up literally buried in our own garbage.

I wonder how long before we go the Japan route? Lifestyles are changing rapidly here too. A growing middle class in India is generating more waste every day. Sure, we recycle more before it ever reaches the dump. But can we congratulate ourselves that our system is 'better'?

I don't think so; not when it's just another way of hiding poverty and masking oppression. Instead we need to realize that waste can never be someone else's problem. It's not about the man or woman who takes the garbage away. It's about us; you and me, as individuals. But even more than that, it's about all of us, collectively. If we don't put our heads together as a society, whether in Japan or India or elsewhere, we'll end up literally buried in our own garbage.

VIEWPOINT 4

In China, Citizens Protest a Garbage Incinerator Project

Wang Pan and Li Jianmin

In China's cities, there is too much trash for the dumps and divided opinions about what to do about it. In this viewpoint, Wang Pan and Li Jianmin, writers for Chinese news agency Xinhua, discuss the controversy surrounding a planned incinerator project in south China. Local residents protested against the plant, citing that both the environment and their property values would be impacted; in response, the government claims drastic measures must be taken to catch up with the piling garbage problem. The authors note that across China, urban areas are facing this dilemma.

As you read, consider the following questions:

1. What are some conflicting arguments between residents and the government concerning incinerator plants?

2. According to Wen Hengfeng, if nothing is done about the garbage problem, how long will it take for all of Beijing's landfills to be full?

3. The Panyu district government has put its incinerator project on hold to do what?

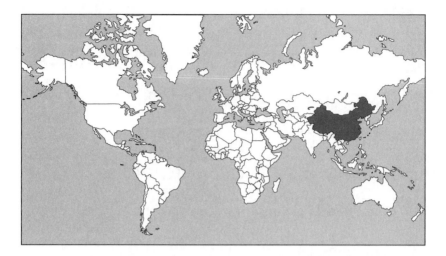

When hundreds of people in a south China city took to the streets earlier this week [November 2009] to protest a planned garbage incinerator project, they highlighted a growing problem for China's booming cities.

The protestors in Guangzhou, capital of Guangdong Province, were demanding the local government scrap the incinerator plant, which, they claimed, would release carcinogens into the air. But for city administrators it meant finding other alternatives to overflowing landfills. "The incineration of household garbage can generate cancer-causing substances like dioxin," resident Guo Lin said. "It is really absurd. How can the government come up with such an idea? More than 300,000 people are living around the proposed incinerator plant."

Opinions Are Divided

The government and residents have been sharply divided on whether to build the plant since late September [2009] when the plan was first unveiled. "The Panyu District is home to 2.5 million people and almost 600,000 tonnes of household garbage are created every year [over 529 lbs. per person per year]. It is predicted that 2,200 tonnes of household garbage will be created every day next year in the district," said Ye Wen, deputy director of the Panyu District Bureau of Urban Utilities and Landscaping. "But our current waste disposal capabilities cannot cope with the increasing amount of household garbage. It is an urgent, practical and inevitable problem," he said.

The new incinerator is planned for the site of a former landfill in Huijiang Village, in Dashi Township, with a designed handling capacity of 2,000 tonnes daily. It would also be a trash-fired power plant. "After years of deliberation, the municipal government has decided to develop trash-fired power plants as they do not occupy much land and can utilize resources very efficiently," said Xu Jianyun, deputy director of the Guangzhou Municipal Committee of Urban Administration. He said the city, with a population of more than 10 million, generates up to 12,000 tonnes of household garbage each day [equally just over 2.5 lbs. of garbage per person per day]. "If new waste treatment facilities are not built, Guangzhou will face a huge garbage crisis over the next two years," he said. Lu Zhiyi, deputy secretary-general of the Guangzhou municipal government and a strong supporter of the incinerator project, dismissed pollution fears. "With modern technology, the waste discharge of the incinerator is able to meet national and international standards, which have been recognized by environmental experts," he said. "The project will not affect the environment and can be accepted."

But residents disagree. "We have collected a great deal of information about waste-to-energy plants on the Internet, in books and field surveys, all showing that they are still heavily polluting and have been abandoned in many countries," resident Zhao Hui said. "We can learn from the experiences of developed countries and solve the problem through garbage classification and landfilling. Why do we have to use incineration?" he said.

In addition to health and pollution fears, residents worry about the values of their properties. "I bought an apartment here a few years ago just because the air quality is better than in downtown areas. If the incinerator is built, it will not only harm everybody's health, but also lead to a plunge in housing prices," resident Lu Ping said.

"We have collected a great deal of information about waste-to-energy plants . . . showing that they are still heavily polluting and have been abandoned in many countries."

The public discontent reached a climax after a press conference by the municipal government over the weekend, during which officials insisted that the construction would go on. That led to the reportedly peaceful protest outside the compound of the municipal government Monday.

Cities Must Do Something with Garbage

It is a dilemma not only for the Panyu District and Guangzhou, but for cities across China, as protests against government plans to build waste incinerators have also been reported in Beijing, Shenzhen and cities in eastern Jiangsu Province earlier this year. "As cities develop quickly, waste disposal has become an increasingly prominent issue in China," said Wen Hengfeng, who is in charge of a plastics-reduction program under the Global Village of Beijing Environmental Education Center, a nongovernmental organization.

Citing government statistics, she said Beijing, with a population of about 17 million, created 18,400 tonnes of garbage every day [just under 2.5 lbs. per person per day], but the city had only a designed disposal capacity of 10,400 tonnes daily and an actual capacity of 17,400 tonnes a day. "All of the city's landfills will be full within four or five years if no measures are to be taken," she said.

Theoretically, the waste discharge of incinerators could be controlled within acceptable limits, but targets would be difficult to maintain in practice due to factors, such as a lack of strict supervision, she said. "From a long-term view, we should make greater efforts to reduce the creation of garbage, strengthen garbage sorting and recycling," she said.

In addition to landfilling, incineration, garbage sorting and recycling, experts have given other alternatives for waste disposal, such as thermal degradation [molecular deterioration of materials (usually organic from heat)], bio-fermentation [anaerobic (without oxygen) cellular process in which organic materials are converted into simpler compounds, creating chemical energy] and chemical means.

"Every method has its advantages and disadvantages. Different areas can choose different ways based on their own conditions," said Li Shaozhen, of the Public Welfare Program Department with the Guangdong Provincial Environmental Protection Foundation, in an interview. For example, landfilling could lead to pollution with the discharge of percolate and harmful gases, she said.

Although thermal degradation and bio-fermentation could have a relatively lower negative impact on the environment, they required high-quality, expensive equipment and massive investment, she said. "In my view, it would be a good choice to combine bio-fermentation, chemical treatment, garbage sorting and recycling in a reasonable way," she said.

Urban Waste Disposal Should Be the Responsibility of All

"The government and public are actually quarreling over many technical issues," said Wang Zechu, a counselor for Guangdong provincial government, when commenting on the protest in Guangzhou. "Both government officials and residents fail to provide convincing environment and health data related to the incinerator. In addition, the two sides have not conducted effective communication," he said.

Burning Toxic Waste Is Dangerous

Burning toxic waste can result in numerous health problems in people. According to the Global Alliance for Incinerator Alternatives/Global Anti-Incinerator Alliance, those health problems can include:

- Cancer

- Heart disease

- Interference of sex organs to unborn fetuses

- Depressed immune system

- Altered liver function

- Skin lesions

- Patchy darkening of skin

- Upper respiratory tract infections

- Reduced IQ

Maore Ithula,
"Kenya: Toxic Smoke Harmful to Foetus's Sex Organs,"
Global Alliance for Incinerator Alternatives/
Global Anti-Incinerator Alliance (GAIA), www.no-burn.org.

Local residents say they should have been invited to discuss the incinerator from the outset when the project was proposed. But government officials say public participation means the public can only join in environmental assessment after the project has been approved by the municipal planning and land authorities. "As the project involves the interests of so many people, the government should fully consider public opinion from the start," Wang said.

This way or another, environmental experts suggest the governments of all Chinese cities should step up efforts in introducing and developing advanced, green technologies in waste disposal. "From a long-term perspective, the government, businesses and public all should be responsible for urban waste disposal," said Prof. Wang Weiping, a specialist on environmental economics from the Beijing-based People's University of China. "The government should—through legislation, supervision and stimulation—encourage businesses to adopt more advanced waste disposal technologies and order environmental authorities to enhance monitoring and protection efforts in the process of waste treatment," he said.

"From a long-term perspective, the government, businesses and public all should be responsible for urban waste disposal."

The Panyu District government has halted the controversial project. "We will launch a half-year consultation process with the public, the media and experts to look for a better way to treat household garbage," said Lou Xukui, head of the Panyu District government. Meanwhile, the Guangzhou Municipal Committee of Urban Administration said government clerks would be sent to every household to solicit opinions. "The government will abide by the openness and transparency principle in choosing the location of the incinerator," said Su Zequn, executive vice mayor of Guangzhou. "We promise the project will not be started if it fails to pass environmental assessment or if it is opposed by the majority of residents," he said.

China's Environmental Mind-Set

Gou Fu Mao

Gou Fu Mao is the Chinese name of Irish journalist Mark Godfrey. In this viewpoint, he discusses how Western chain businesses encourage a throwaway culture in China. Paradoxically, Irishborn Mao is met with comments on Westerners' environmental friendliness whenever he brings his own cup or bag to businesses; the fact that Starbucks, McDonald's, and other Western chains make it exceedingly difficult to not use their disposable tableware, on the other hand, is not noted. According to Mao, it is on the streets of China—where professional recyclers sift through trash—that China's environmentalism comes through.

As you read, consider the following questions:

1. According to Mao, how do Western chains encourage a throwaway culture in China?
2. What difference does Mao notice in street vendors versus those working in Western chains?
3. Why is Zhang earning about 60 percent of what he used to make?

I usually feel good about the march of environmentalism in China: People here, on average, consume less and, compared to other developing nations I've been to, are more aware

Gou Fu Mao, "Recycling Mentality," *Beijing Review*, vol. 52, no. 8. February 26, 2009.

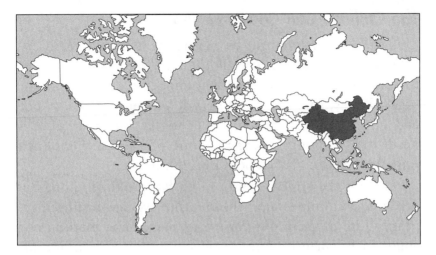

of the damaged mess our environment is in. But it annoys me to see Western coffee and fast-food chains come to China. While paying lip service to the community through expensive corporate social responsibility campaigns, they inculcate a throwaway culture in local customers by offering only throwaway tableware.

I've stopped going to my local Starbucks because the staff will only reluctantly pour my coffee using porcelain mugs— tucked away in a cupboard—and by default serve in disposable plastic-coated paper cups. There's a 2-yuan ($0.3) discount if you bring your own mug, but this incentive isn't publicized, at least not prominently, in store.

Similarly at Chinese branches of KFC [Kentucky Fried Chicken] and McDonald's: Several times I gave an attendant my own coffee cup (explaining that I don't want to generate waste) and each time they poured the coffee first into a throwaway plastic cup. That defeats the purpose of bringing my own reusable dishware (which also saves the fast-food shop the cost and task of dumping theirs). "I'm being environmentally friendly," I've tried saying. Sometimes there's a nod of recognition but often it's a giggle or a quizzical stare of bemusement.

The Chinese Can Conserve Too

Aren't these people taught by management to save resources? Does KFC and McDonald's talk to staff about saving resources to save the planet (and company money)? Excess milk and sugar sachets, handed out by default whether wanted or not, end up in the bin, unused. Better to ask customers if they need milk and sugar, because some of us don't. For their wastefulness I now avoid both establishments.

Out on the streets there's more hope. While China has perilous environmental challenges, the average Beijinger appears aware of these. Vendors in local morning markets nod approvingly, when I refuse plastic and proffer a cloth bag. My action is praised to other customers. "Westerners are more environment friendly than Chinese" is a phrase I've come to know.

That's not necessarily true. "Chinese people can also conserve," I usually reply. And many do, partly because there's an incentive and partly because there's no choice. Because China's resources are limited compared to its almost infinitely large population, it's a lot easier to save and reuse resources here. I particularly like how Beijing's streets are patrolled by professional recyclers who cheerfully sift trash for paper, plastic and glass.

"Westerners are more environment friendly than Chinese" is a phrase I've come to know.

Other Recycling Methods

They're excited to come upon electronic appliances, which can be cranked up to reuse—or gutted for valuable copper wires. The bins on our street are emptied of their reusables by Zhang, a small-town man from northern Hebei Province. "Paper and plastic are not waste, they are reusable stuff that just needs to be picked up," he likes to say each time I call him to collect a stack of paper I've hoarded. My retired neighbor starts his day with a sweep of the local McDonald's and KFC stores. "After breakfast there's a lot of newspaper left lying around on tables," he explains. He sells his stash to Zhang, who tells me these days he's getting 0.09 yuan per ($0.01) plastic bottle and 1 yuan ($0.14) per kilogram of newspapers—about 60 percent what he was being paid a year ago.

The current economic climate changes everything. Prices for recyclables have fallen by up to 70 percent. Last year [2008] plastic bottles (squashed and shaved into droplets) cost about half what a manufacturer would pay for virgin plastic—high because of the high price of oil.

Now a world in recession doesn't need so many plastic dinner sets and polyester tracksuits. Hence manufacturers don't need the recycled plastics and folks like Zhang get paid less for their bottles. It's a similar story for the newspapers he's been collecting: Chinese paper mills aren't buying new stocks because newspapers and magazines drop sales and advertising (hence use less pages) in a recession.

It shows how interdependent and hooked up the global environment, as well as our economy, is. It's tough times for Zhang and his colleagues. But they're still collecting, figuring there'll be an upturn in prices, eventually. My local Starbucks meanwhile continues to throwaway cups that no one can reuse. Cheers for Zhang.

In South Asia, Many Ships
Meet Their Toxic Death

Jacob Baynham

What happens to aging ships? According to writer Jacob Baynham in this viewpoint, many are destined for the shipping scrap yards in South Asia. Once there, the ships are torn apart so the steel can be reused. The problem environmental groups and others have with this method, Baynham reports, concerns the way in which the ships are dismantled. He notes that South Asia's limited regulations and cheap labor lead to dangerous conditions for workers and for the environment: Each year, workers die and toxins are released into the sea.

As you read, consider the following questions:

1. Why do environmental groups think the *Anders* and the *Bonny* are heading for the ship scrap yard?
2. What happens to the toxic materials of scrapped ships once they are dismantled?
3. What does the Toxic Substances Control Act of 1976 prohibit?

When the 30-year-old cargo ship MV *Anders* cruised out of Norfolk, Va., at 11 p.m. on Wednesday, Aug. 26, it may have been sailing through one of the largest loopholes in U.S. maritime regulations.

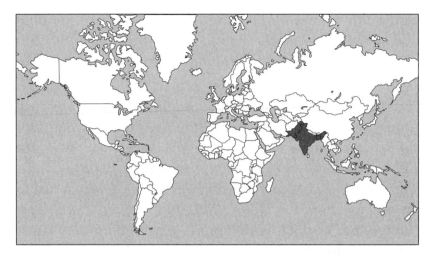

Three weeks earlier, the *Anders* was a U.S.-flagged vessel called the MVP *Pfc. James Anderson Jr.*, named for a young Marine who saved his platoon members' lives by falling on a Viet Cong grenade. It had hauled cargo for the U.S. Navy for more than two decades and was now retiring. The ship's new owners, Star Maritime Corp., had renamed it the *Anders*, painted over the excess letters on the hull, and raised the flag of its new registry—the Caribbean nation of St. Kitts and Nevis. The *Anders* left Virginia empty.

Its 29-year-old sister ship, the MV *Bonny* (formerly the MV *1st Lt. Alex Bonnyman*), followed two days later under the same flag and ownership. The Coast Guard listed the ships' next port of call as Santos, Brazil. But environmental groups, trade journals, and industry watchdogs claim the ultimate destination for these aging vessels will be the Dickensian scrap yards of Bangladesh.

The *Anders* and the *Bonny* served in the U.S. Navy's Military Sealift Command for 24 years. Stationed at Diego Garcia in the Indian Ocean, they delivered military cargo during both Iraq wars, as well as Operation Restore Hope in Somalia. But the Navy never actually owned the ships. They chartered them from Wilmington Trust, which sold them to Star Maritime

119

earlier this summer. When Star Maritime renamed the ships and submitted an application to reflag them under St. Kitts and Nevis registration, environmental groups recognized the telltale signs of vessels about to be scrapped and cried foul.

The Basel Action Network, a Seattle-based environmental group leading the campaign to stop the export of old ships for scrap, monitors old vessels in U.S. waters and alerts the EPA when their owners attempt to recycle them overseas. There are several reliable warning signs. First, a ship is sold to an obscure company (which U.S. ship-breakers call a "Last Voyage Inc."), which is sometimes a subsidiary of a larger company active in the scrapping business. Then it is renamed and registered under another nation's flag before sailing to South Asia.

Most of the world's old ships are sent to die on the shores of India, Pakistan, and Bangladesh.

"It's outrageous that these ships were allowed to sail," says Colby Self, director of BAN's Green Ship Recycling campaign. "In a sense, they were government vessels." But once the ships' contracts had expired, all legal responsibilities lay with their owners.

Most of the world's old ships are sent to die on the shores of India, Pakistan, and Bangladesh. Vessels are beached there at high tide and cut into pieces by teams of poorly paid migrant workers. Heavy equipment and cranes are inoperable on the sand, so workers dismantle the ships by removing large portions, which drop to the beach. They use fire torches to cut through steel hulls—even those of old oil tankers. Dozens of workers die each year from explosions, falling steel, and disease. As for the asbestos, polychlorinated biphenyls (PCBs), tributyltin (TBT), and other toxic materials onboard the old ships, much of it washes out to sea. (PCBs and TBT are persistent organic pollutants that work their way up the marine food chain and damage the nervous systems of large mammals.)

If the *Anders* and *Bonny* are headed to Bangladesh, they won't be alone. South Asia's ship-breaking yards are experiencing an ironic boom in the middle of the global recession. Ship owners faced with shrinking cargo volumes are culling their fleets by scrapping old vessels rather than paying for them to sit empty. South Asia's yards, which take advantage of cheap labor, scant regulations, and high regional demand for steel, will buy a vessel for twice the price a U.S. ship-breaker could offer. In Bangladesh, ships like the *Anders* and *Bonny* (which are two-and-a-half football fields long and weigh more than 23,000 tons) are worth at least $7 million apiece.

In 1998, the Clinton administration slapped a moratorium on scrapping U.S.-flagged vessels overseas after the *Baltimore Sun* ran a Pulitzer Prize–winning string of stories about the conditions of the South Asian scrap yards. But ship owners have dozens of so-called "flags of convenience" at their disposal to circumvent the ban. Most of these flags belong to small, poor countries with little maritime oversight—places like St. Kitts and Nevis.

Ship owners submit their reflagging requests to the U.S. Maritime Administration (MARAD), which considers whether the ships would be needed for national security in the event of war. For old vessels, this is seldom the case. MARAD began alerting the EPA of old ships attempting to reflag after the SS *Oceanic*, a former Norwegian cruise liner, slipped out of San Francisco last year with almost 500 tons of asbestos and PCBs onboard.

The Toxic Substances Control Act of 1976 prohibits the export of PCBs, asbestos, and lead-based paint—materials often used in the paint, cabling, and gaskets of older ships because of their fire-retardant qualities. If the EPA suspects a vessel applying for reflagging contains hazardous materials, it

The Toxicity of Scrapped Ships

Environmental groups such as the Basel Action Network (BAN) and Greenpeace are fighting to end the irresponsible scrapping of old vessels for good reason. The table below includes the toxic substances found on scrapped ships.

Substance	Location	Ship Scrapping Dangers	Health/Environmental Concerns
Asbestos	Found between steel plates and doors; once disturbed, it breaks into dust and fibers which stay in the air for long periods of time.	In many ship scrap yards, its dust is present. Workers handle asbestos fibers without masks or gloves.	Prolonged contact leads to permanent breathing difficulties such as asbestosis, lung cancer.
Heavy metals, including lead, mercury, and iron	In paints, coatings, anodes and electrical equipment.	Is often tossed away by workers not wearing protective equipment. These metals are often dumped and burnt on beaches, leading to widespread pollution.	Can cause cancer, paralysis, and retardation in young children.
POPs (Persistent Organic Pollutants)	Generated as by-products of industrial/combustion processes, such as by burning toxic waste.	Waste, including toxic waste, is burned in open fires in many ship scrap yards.	Highly toxic, causing death, birth defects, and diseases including cancer, allergies, and nervous/immune system disorders. Can persist in the atmosphere for decades.

continued

The Toxicity of Scrapped Ships [CONTINUED]

Oil and sludge	Inside ships' pipes and tanks.	Poisons marine wildlife and their habitat and can be consumed in contaminated fish or water. Toxic to humans, whether consumed or inhaled.
Bilge and ballast water	**Bilge:** In water that has been heavily contaminated with oil and cargo residues and drained down to ship storage; **Ballast:** In water that has been brought on board to adjust the ship's stability.	Waste oil is often burned on the shore and dumped into the sea. In addition to health dangers, this poses dangers of fires and explosions.
		Is often carelessly dumped into seas once ships are scrapped.
		Pollutes coastal areas, threatening marine wildlife and their habitat, as well as humans who consume fish in the area.

TAKEN FROM: "Toxic Substances on Board Ships," Greenpeace. http://www.greenpeace.org/india/campaigns/toxics-free-future/ship-breaking/problems-of-ship-breaking/toxic-substances-on-board-ship; "What Are POPs?" http://web.worldbank.org/WBSITE/EXTERNAL/TOPICS/ENVIRONMENT/EXTPOPS/0,,contentMDK:20487948~menuPK:1165797~pagePK:148956~piPK:216618~theSitePK:408121,00.html.

can order that vessel to be tested. But because ships are not required to inventory these materials, and the EPA has limited time and resources to devote to every old ship, environmentalists contend that each year many vessels slip through the cracks.

"When we scrap a ship, we must assume it has hazardous material onboard until we can prove otherwise."

In the case of the *Bonny* and *Anders*, EPA spokesman David Sternberg says, "Based on the available information, the EPA has no sufficient reason to contain these ships." Sternberg adds that the EPA received a letter from the new owners insisting the vessels will be used in trade and will not be scrapped.

This seems unlikely to Kevin McCabe, founder of International Shipbreaking Ltd. in Texas. He says buying two cargo ships at the end of their life spans for their utilitarian purposes alone would "belie the economics of the market today." McCabe is convinced that the *Bonny* and *Anders* will be scrapped in Asia. And he doesn't think they're clean, either. "I'll bet you dollars to doughnuts that there are PCBs on those ships," he says. "No question about it." The EPA would be singing a different tune if the ships were to be dismantled at his Brownsville recycling facility, he adds. "When we scrap a ship, we must assume it has hazardous material onboard until we can prove otherwise."

Colby Self of BAN says he's disappointed that the Obama administration could so easily let these ships slip away. "[The EPA] made a calculated decision based on their low-risk assessment, and they let them go," he says. Under the Bush administration, the EPA was very diligent in following up on BAN's warnings, he says.

But Self isn't giving up hope that the ships can be stopped before they wash up on South Asian shores. "We will be warning Bangladesh to bar the entry of these renegade vessels," he says. "This story is far from over."

Periodical Bibliography

The following articles have been selected to supplement the diverse views presented in this chapter.

Chris Barton and Tracey Barnett — "Plastic Not Fantastic," *New Zealand Herald*, January 9, 2010.

Max Borders — "Burning Gas to Save Glass," *Washington Examiner*, April 22, 2010.

Daily Telegraph — "In NSW It's Not Easy or Cheap Being Green," January 4, 2010.

Jason Dearen — "Rotting Ships to Be Removed from Suisun Bay," Associated Press, March 31, 2010.

Greenpeace — "Dell Targeted for Breaking Promise on Toxic Chemicals," March 29, 2010. www.greenpeace.org.

Umesh Isalkar — "Villagers to Again Block Dumping of Garbage," *Times of India*, December 22, 2009.

Andrew Leonard — "The Final Word on Recycling," *Salon*, January 24, 2007.

Los Angeles Times — "Paper or Plastic or Neither," April 16, 2010.

Richard Morrison — "Recycled Rubbish: Something Doesn't Smell Quite Right," *Times* (London), April 4, 2006.

Ruth Mortimer — "Why Recycling Isn't the Way to Clean Up," *Marketing Week*, April 22, 2010.

Mother Jones — "MoJo Forum: Is Recycling a Waste?" April 20, 2009.

Kate Sheppard — "Fair and . . . Carbon Neutral?" *Mother Jones*, April 23, 2010.

GLOBALVIEWPOINTS

CHAPTER 3

Conventional Solutions to the Garbage and Recycling Dilemma

In the United States and Around the World, Plastic Bags Must Go

Katharine Mieszkowski

In this viewpoint Katharine Mieszkowski, a senior writer for Salon, demonstrates all that is wrong with plastic bags. From its oil-dependent birth to its years spent littering the landscape, and finally, to its resilience to ever go away (either through decomposition or recycling), she makes it clear that everything is wrong with the plastic bag. Additionally, plastic bags kill over a million birds and one hundred thousand marine mammals and sea turtles every year. Around the world, countries and cities are trying to find ways to cope with the problem of plastic bags.

As you read, consider the following questions:

1. What percentage of plastic bags are recycled in the United States and worldwide?

2. Why can't San Francisco's Recycle Center recycle plastic bags?

3. Why is it unusual for a plastic bag to be recycled into another plastic bag?

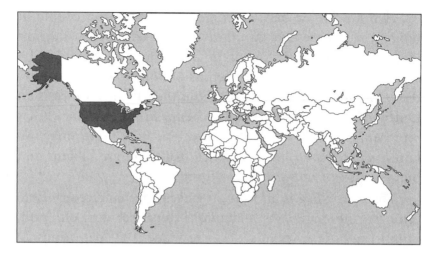

Aug. 10, 2007—On a foggy Tuesday morning, kids out of school for summer break are learning to sail on the waters of Lake Merritt. A great egret hunts for fish, while dozens of cormorants perch, drying their wings. But we're not here to bird-watch or go boating. Twice a week volunteers with the Lake Merritt Institute gather on these shores of the nation's oldest national wildlife refuge to fish trash out of the water, and one of their prime targets is plastic bags. Armed with gloves and nets with long handles, like the kind you'd use to fish leaves out of a backyard swimming pool, we take to the shores to seek our watery prey.

Dr. Richard Bailey, executive director of the institute, is most concerned about the bags that get waterlogged and sink to the bottom. "We have a lot of animals that live on the bottom: shrimp, shellfish, sponges," he says. "It's like you're eating at your dinner table and somebody comes along and throws a plastic tarp over your dinner table and you."

This morning, a turtle feeds serenely next to a half submerged Walgreens bag. The bag looks ghostly, ethereal even, floating, as if in some kind of purgatory suspended between its briefly useful past and its none-too-promising future. A bright blue bag floats just out of reach, while a duck cruises by. Here's a Ziploc bag, there a Safeway bag. In a couple of hours, I fish more than two dozen plastic bags out of the lake with my net, along with cigarette butts, candy wrappers and a soccer ball. As we work, numerous passersby on the popular trail that circles the urban lake shout their thanks, which is an undeniable boost. Yet I can't help being struck that our efforts represent a tiny drop in the ocean. If there's one thing we know about these plastic bags, it's that there are billions and billions more where they came from.

The plastic bag is an icon of convenience culture, by some estimates the single most ubiquitous consumer item on Earth, numbering in the trillions. They're made from petroleum or natural gas with all the attendant environmental impacts of harvesting fossil fuels. One recent study found that the inks and colorants used on some bags contain lead, a toxin. Every year, Americans throw away some 100 billion plastic bags after they've been used to transport a prescription home from the drugstore or a quart of milk from the grocery store. It's equivalent to dumping nearly 12 million barrels of oil.

If there's one thing we know about these plastic bags, it's that there are billions and billions more where they came from.

Only 1 percent of plastic bags are recycled worldwide—about 2 percent in the U.S.—and the rest, when discarded, can persist for centuries. They can spend eternity in landfills, but that's not always the case. "They're so aerodynamic that even when they're properly disposed of in a trash can they can still blow away and become litter," says Mark Murray, executive director of Californians Against Waste. It's as litter that plastic bags have the most baleful effect. And we're not talking about your everyday eyesore.

Once aloft, stray bags cartwheel down city streets, alight in trees, billow from fences like flags, clog storm drains, wash into rivers and bays and even end up in the ocean, washed out to sea. Bits of plastic bags have been found in the nests of albatrosses in the remote Midway Islands. Floating bags can look all too much like tasty jellyfish to hungry marine critters. According to the Blue Ocean Society for Marine Conservation, more than a million birds and 100,000 marine mammals and sea turtles die every year from eating or getting entangled in plastic. The conservation group estimates that 50 percent of all marine litter is some form of plastic. There are 46,000 pieces of plastic litter floating in every square mile of ocean, according to the United Nations Environment Programme. In the Northern Pacific Gyre, a great vortex of ocean currents, there's now a swirling mass of plastic trash about 1,000 miles off the coast of California, which spans an area that's twice the size of Texas, including fragments of plastic bags. There's six times as much plastic as biomass, including plankton and jellyfish, in the gyre. "It's an endless stream of incessant plastic particles everywhere you look," says Dr. Marcus Eriksen, director of education and research for the Algalita Marine Research Foundation, which studies plastics in the marine environment. "Fifty or 60 years ago, there was no plastic out there."

Following the lead of countries like Ireland, Bangladesh, South Africa, Thailand and Taiwan, some U.S. cities are striking back against what they see as an expensive, wasteful and unnecessary mess. This year, San Francisco and Oakland outlawed the use of plastic bags in large grocery stores and pharmacies, permitting only paper bags with at least 40 percent recycled content or otherwise compostable bags. The bans have not taken effect yet, but already the city of Oakland is being sued by an association of plastic bag manufacturers calling itself the Coalition to Support Plastic Bag Recycling. Meanwhile, other communities across the country, including Santa Monica, Calif., New Haven, Conn., Annapolis, Md., and Portland, Ore., are considering taking drastic legislative action against the bags. In Ireland, a now 22-cent tax on plastic bags has slashed their use by more than 90 percent since 2002. In flood-prone Bangladesh, where plastic bags choked drainage systems, the bags have been banned since 2002.

The problem with plastic bags isn't just where they end up, it's that they never seem to end. "All the plastic that has been made is still around in smaller and smaller pieces," says Stephanie Barger, executive director of the Earth Resource Foundation, which has undertaken a Campaign Against the Plastic Plague. Plastic doesn't biodegrade. That means unless they've been incinerated—a noxious proposition—every plastic bag you've ever used in your entire life, including all those bags that the newspaper arrives in on your doorstep, even on cloudless days when there isn't a sliver of a chance of rain, still exists in some form, even fragmented bits, and will exist long after you're dead.

Grand efforts are under way to recycle plastic bags, but so far those efforts have resulted mostly in a mass of confusion. A tour of Recycle Central in San Francisco makes it easy to see why. The plant is a Willie Wonka factory of refuse. Located on a bay pier with a stunning view of the downtown skyline, some 700 tons of discarded annual reports, Rolling Rock bottles, Diet Coke cans, Amazon.com cardboard boxes, Tide plastic detergent bottles and StarKist tuna fish cans surge into this warehouse every weekday, dumped from trucks into a great clattering, shifting mound. The building tinkles and thumps with the sound of thousands of pounds of glass, aluminum, paper, plastic and cardboard knocking together, as all this detritus passes through a dizzying network of conveyor belts, spinning disks, magnets and gloved human hands to emerge as 16 different sorted, recyclable commodities, baled up by the ton to be shipped or trucked away and made into something new again. It's one way that the city of San Francisco manages to divert some 69 percent of its waste from landfills. But this city's vaunted recycling program, which is so advanced that it can collect coffee grounds and banana peels from urbanites' apartment kitchens and transform them into compost used to grow grapes in Napa Valley vineyards, simply cannot master the plastic bag.

Ask John Jurinek, the plant manager at Recycle Central, what's wrong with plastic bags and he has a one-word answer: "Everything." Plastic bags, of which San Franciscans use some 180 million per year, cannot be recycled here. Yet the hopeful arrow symbol emblazoned on the bags no doubt inspires lots of residents to toss their used ones into the blue recycling bin, feeling good that they've done the right thing. But that symbol on all kinds of plastic items by no means guarantees they can be recycled curbside. (The plastic bags collected at the recycling plant are trucked to the regular dump.) By chucking their plastic bags in the recycling, what those well-meaning San Franciscans have done is throw a plastic wrench into the city's grand recycling factory. If you want to recycle a plastic bag it's better to bring it back to the store where you got it.

As the great mass of recyclables moves past the initial sort deck on a series of spinning disks, stray plastic bags clog the machinery. It's such a problem that one machine is shut down while a worker wearing kneepads and armed with a knife spends an hour climbing precariously on the disks to cut the bags out, yielding a Medusa's hair-mass of wrenched and twisted plastic. In the middle of the night, when the vast sorting operation grinds to a halt to prepare for the next 700-ton day, two workers will spend hours at this dirty job.

Ask John Jurinek, the plant manager at Recycle Central, what's wrong with plastic bags and he has a one-word answer: "Everything."

Some states are attacking the recycling problem by trying to encourage shoppers to take the bags back to grocery stores. California requires large grocery stores and pharmacies that distribute the bags known in the trade as T-shirt bags—those common polyethylene bags with two handles, usually made from petroleum or natural gas—to take them back for recycling, and to print instructions on the bags to encourage shoppers to return them to the stores. San Francisco Department of the Environment spokesperson Mark Westlund, who can see plastic bags lodged in the trees on Market Street from his second-story office window, is skeptical about the state's ability to get shoppers to take back their bags. "We've had in-store recycling in San Francisco for over 10 years, and it's never really been successful," says Westlund, who estimates that the city achieved only a 1 percent recycling rate of plastic bags at the stores. "People have to pack up the bags, bring them into the store and drop them off. I think you'd be more inclined to bring your own bag than do that."

Regardless, polyethylene plastic bags are recyclable, says Howie Fendley, a senior environmental chemist for MBDC, an ecological design firm. "It's a matter of getting the feedstock to the point where a recycler can economically justify taking those bags and recycling them. The problem is they're mostly air. There has to be a system in place where they get a nice big chunk of polyethylene that can be mechanically ground, melted and then re-extruded."

So far that system nationwide consists mainly of supermarkets and superstores like Wal-Mart voluntarily stockpiling the bags brought back in by conscientious shoppers, and selling them to recyclers or plastic brokers, who in turn sell them to recyclers. In the U.S., one company buys half of the used plastic bags available on the open market in the United States, using about 1.5 billion plastic bags per year. That's Trex, based in Winchester, Va., which makes composite decking out of the bags and recycled wood. It takes some 2,250 plastic bags to make a single 16-foot-long, 2-inch-by-6-inch plank. It might feel good to buy decking made out of something that otherwise could have choked a sea turtle, but not so fast. That use is not an example of true recycling, points out Carol Missel-

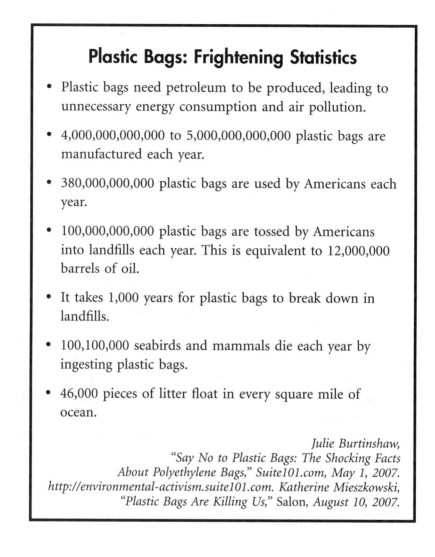

Plastic Bags: Frightening Statistics

- Plastic bags need petroleum to be produced, leading to unnecessary energy consumption and air pollution.

- 4,000,000,000,000 to 5,000,000,000,000 plastic bags are manufactured each year.

- 380,000,000,000 plastic bags are used by Americans each year.

- 100,000,000,000 plastic bags are tossed by Americans into landfills each year. This is equivalent to 12,000,000 barrels of oil.

- It takes 1,000 years for plastic bags to break down in landfills.

- 100,100,000 seabirds and mammals die each year by ingesting plastic bags.

- 46,000 pieces of litter float in every square mile of ocean.

Julie Burtinshaw,
"Say No to Plastic Bags: The Shocking Facts
About Polyethylene Bags," Suite101.com, May 1, 2007.
http://environmental-activism.suite101.com. Katherine Mieszkowski,
"Plastic Bags Are Killing Us," Salon, August 10, 2007.

dine, sustainability coordinator for the city of Oakland. "We're not recycling plastic bags into plastic bags," she says. "They're being downcycled, meaning that they're being put into another product that itself can never be recycled."

Unlike a glass beer bottle or an aluminum can, it's unusual that a plastic bag is made back into another plastic bag, because it's typically more expensive than just making a new plastic bag. After all, the major appeal of plastic bags to stores is that they're much cheaper than paper. Plastic bags cost grocery stores under 2 cents per bag, while paper goes for 4 to 6 cents and compostable bags 9 to 14 cents. However, says Eriksen from the Algalita Marine Research Foundation, "The long-term cost of having these plastic bags blowing across our landscape, across our beaches and accumulating in the northern Pacific far outweighs the short-term loss to a few."

"I haven't heard about the oil guys growing more oil lately."

Of course, shoppers could just bring their own canvas bags, and avoid the debate altogether. The California bag recycling law also requires stores to sell reusable bags. Yet it will be a sad irony if outlawing the bags, as San Francisco and Oakland have, doesn't inspire shoppers to bring their own canvas bags, but simply sends them to paper bags, which come with their own environmental baggage. In fact, plastic bags were once thought to be an ecologically friendly alternative to cutting down trees to make paper ones. It takes 14 million trees to produce the 10 billion paper grocery bags used every year by Americans, according to the Natural Resources Defense Council. Yet suggesting that plastic bags made out of petroleum are a better choice burns up Barger from the Earth Resources Foundation. "People say, 'I'm using plastic. I'm saving trees,'" she says. "But have you ever seen what Shell, Mobil and Chevron are doing down in the rain forests to get oil?"

Gordon Bennett, an executive in the San Francisco Bay chapter of the Sierra Club, agrees. "The fundamental thing about trees is that if you manage them properly they're a renewable resource," he says. "I haven't heard about the oil guys growing more oil lately." Still, as the plastic bag industry never tires of pointing out, paper bags are heavier than plastic bags, so they take more fossil fuels to transport. Some life cycle assessments have put plastic bags out ahead of paper, when it comes to energy and waste in the manufacturing process. But paper bags with recycled content, like those soon to be required in San Francisco and Oakland, use less energy and produce less waste than those made from virgin paper.

The only salient answer to paper or plastic is neither. Bring a reusable canvas bag, says Darby Hoover, a senior resource specialist for the Natural Resources Defense Council. However, if you have to make a choice between the two, she recommends taking whichever bag you're more likely to reuse the most times, since, like many products, the production of plastic or paper bags has the biggest environmental impact, not the disposal of them. "Reusing is a better option because it avoids the purchase of another product."

The only salient answer to paper or plastic is neither.

Some stores, like IKEA, have started trying to get customers to bring their own bags by charging them 5 cents per plastic bag. The Swedish furniture company donates the proceeds from the bag sales to a conservation group. Another solution just might be fashion. Bringing your own bag—or BYOB as Whole Foods dubs it—is the latest eco-chic statement. When designer Anya Hindmarch's "I am not a plastic bag" bag hit stores in Taiwan, there was so much demand for the limited edition bag that the riot police had to be called in to control a stampede, which sent 30 people to the hospital.

In Australia, a Small Town Bans Bottled Water

Warren McLaren

In this viewpoint Warren McLaren, a writer and ecologist from Sydney, celebrates a small Australian town, Bundanoon, for becoming the first bottled water–free town. The proposal was community sparked and endorsed, demonstrating how local communities can quickly and efficiently make decisions. To make up for the lack of bottled water, Bundanoon businesses will sell reusable water bottles and the town will install three filtered water stations. McLaren also discusses the problems with bottled water, including environmental hazards and cost. Additionally, bottled water is often tap water in disguise.

As you read, consider the following questions:

1. How did Bundanoon pass the bottled water ban?
2. What kind of public response followed Bundanoon's bottle water ban?
3. What are some of the problems associated with bottled water?

An Australian country town, Bundanoon, has voted at a community hall meeting to overwhelmingly support a proposal that it become Australia's (if not the world's) first bottled water free town.

Warren McLaren, "Community Votes to Become Australia's First Bottled Water Free Town," TreeHugger, August 7, 2009. Reproduced by permission. www.treehugger.com.

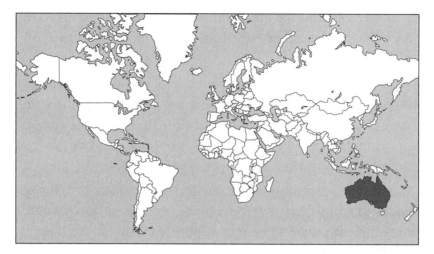

And the news seems to have spurred on the Australian state of New South Wales (NSW) to announce a ban on bottled water from all state offices and agencies.

Community Action

The idea was raised in an open letter to the town's community newspaper and immediately a working group of local residents from the New South Wales town of Bundanoon rallied around the concept. They developed the concept further, giving it the slogan of Bundy On Tap and approached local retail businesses and events to see if they would support the initiative.

This is community spirit at its most engaged. A town's people making their own decisions, and taking localised action on environmental issues.

A meeting of about 20 local businesses endorsed the project, even though about half of them, as beverage retailers, stood to lose income from the venture. But they magnanimously recognised the environmental impact of bottled water, and felt, on balance, the benefit to the community outweighed the sales profit.

At a town meeting on Wednesday 8 July 09 an estimated 400 local people (from a town of about 2,500) filled the community hall, and after a discussion on the pros and cons of the venture, they voted wholeheartedly for the proposal. It is understood there were 1 to 2 persons not in favour.

This is community spirit at its most engaged. A town's people making their own decisions, and taking localised action on environmental issues, without waiting for outside external forces to do the work for them.

Implementation of Bottled Water Free Town

So how will the proposal work in practice? Well, the town's retail businesses that previously sold single-use, bottled still water will no longer stock this product in their drink fridges. (Sparkling water, fruit juices, etc., are not affected because they are not available via the municipal water system.) Shops will alternatively make available for sale affordable, reusable, refillable water bottles. Some are even considering the option of in-store chilled water filters, so customers can access filtered water for their reusable bottles.

Additionally, with the assistance of the Bottled Water Alliance, a campaign of the activist organisation Do Something, the town will partner with Street Furniture Australia and Culligan to install three filtered water 'bubblers' or water stations. Two for the town and another for the town's primary school. The water stations will be prominently sign-posted, and will also incorporate taps that can be used for refilling bottles. It is anticipated that most of these endeavours will be realised by October 2009, making Bundanoon effectively Australia's first bottled water free town.

Topical Issue

As news broke in newspapers on the morning of Bundanoon's pending vote, media interest became intense. We understand that almost 80 interviews were given during the day and not just to Australian media, although three of the major TV stations immediately sent crews to cover the news. International media from the UK, New Zealand, the USA and even Japan picked up on the story. Obviously bottled water is an issue that captures hearts and minds. And can polarize opinion. (See the comments that accompany the many stories—some listed below—we've previously covered on bottled water. [not shown])

Environmental Impact of Bottled Water

In information compiled by the town's Bundy On Tap campaign, they note that Australia's annual consumption of bottled water is about 540 million litres. To sell this much bottled water the industry uses approximately 1 billion litres of water each year. In environmental terms the production and distribution of this volume of bottled water created more than 60,000 tonnes of greenhouse gas emissions, equivalent to the emissions 13,000 cars generate in one year.

The NSW Department of Environment, Climate Change estimates that 200ml of oil is used to produce, package, transport and refrigerate each litre bottle of bottled water. As a result, at least 50 million litres of oil are used in the manufacture and distribution of bottled water in Australia every year. Thus bottled water has a higher carbon footprint, that is more than 300 times greater per litre than tap water.

A comprehensive American study found the total energy required for bottled water production was as much as 2,000 times the energy cost of producing tap water. Much of that energy, in the form of plastic created from limited oil reserves,

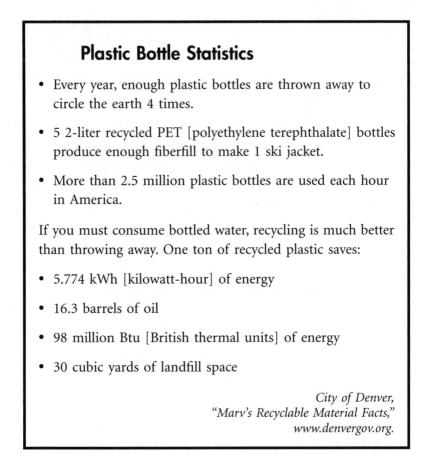

Plastic Bottle Statistics

- Every year, enough plastic bottles are thrown away to circle the earth 4 times.

- 5 2-liter recycled PET [polyethylene terephthalate] bottles produce enough fiberfill to make 1 ski jacket.

- More than 2.5 million plastic bottles are used each hour in America.

If you must consume bottled water, recycling is much better than throwing away. One ton of recycled plastic saves:

- 5.774 kWh [kilowatt-hour] of energy

- 16.3 barrels of oil

- 98 million Btu [British thermal units] of energy

- 30 cubic yards of landfill space

City of Denver,
"Marv's Recyclable Material Facts,"
www.denvergov.org.

is squandered as up to 65% of single use bottles used for commercial bottled water in Australia are not recycled, finding their way into landfills or waterways.

Yet bottled water costs 500 times more than the water readily available from municipally provided taps. In many cases, it is, in fact, the same water. Many millions of litres of bottled water sold in Australia are sourced from municipal water. Nor is bottled water necessarily any more safe. In Australia bacteria, chemical disinfectants and aluminum have been found in bottled water samples.

State Government Endorsement

Not long after the news of Bundanoon's Bundy On Tap project was unveiled, such startling figures were also being quoted by the NSW State Premier, Nathan Rees, who announced a state-wide ban on the provision of bottled water through all state-run buildings and agencies.

In the United States and Beyond, Food Service Must Address Waste Management

Andrew Shakman

Andrew Shakman is president and CEO of LeanPath Inc., a technology company providing automated food waste tracking systems to the food service industry. In this viewpoint, Shakman provides details about how food service operators can reduce their waste, including food and packaging waste. Reducing wastes not only cuts costs for businesses, he asserts, but it also positively impacts the environment. Shakman contends that whether or not food service operators feel ready to embrace new waste management techniques, they are an inevitable part of the future and will benefit both businesses and the environment.

As you read, consider the following questions:

1. What are the three leading waste management issues to emerge in food service operation?
2. According to the viewpoint, what is the definition of "zero waste"?
3. What are some options for on-site food waste processing?

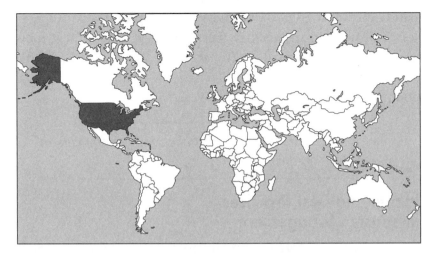

Once upon a time, the topic of waste management conjured images of messy garbage handling, hauling and processing. Most foodservice operators viewed it as largely unrelated to their core business. Not unlike electricity or water utilities, you signed a hauling contract and checked the task off your list.

But with these challenging economic times—and in a society increasingly focused on sustainability—it's no longer advisable for operators to treat waste as a peripheral concern. We spend massive dollars to purchase food and supplies that become waste and our discards make a huge, negative impact on both our financial results and the environment. Cutting waste makes sense—and it also happens to be one of the least painful ways to remove costs, avoiding the negative shockwaves of staff reductions or menu changes.

For these reasons, foodservice operators should make waste management one of their top priorities. This starts by redefining their thought processes to recognize that waste management is not about garbage—it's about reforming inefficient policies, procedures, and behaviors that lead to many types of waste. Managing a foodservice operation's waste cannot be delegated to a facilities manager or waste hauler; it requires hands-on knowledge of foodservice and production. Operators will need to master new best practices, deploy new tools and build new partnerships to usher in a new era of high efficiency and low waste. The following are trends to watch and concepts to master in 2010.

Foodservice operators should make waste management one of their top priorities.

Identifying Best Practices in Waste Management

Foodservice operators have many potential waste management issues to address. Three leading issues have emerged in most waste management plans as primary considerations worthy of initial and sustained attention:

Pre-Consumer Food Waste. Also known as kitchen waste, pre-consumer food waste includes all food discarded by foodservice staff before it reaches a guest, including overproduced and expired items, spoilage, trim waste and waste due to handling errors such as contamination, dropping and burning. Pre-consumer food waste typically equals 4 percent to 10 percent of the total food purchased.

Post-Consumer Food Waste. Also known as plate waste, post-consumer food waste is all food discarded by guests. This waste stream needs to be managed in a completely different manner than pre-consumer food waste because the reasons for its creation are quite different. While production and service behaviors primarily drive pre-consumer food waste, guest discretion heavily influences post-consumer food waste. Proper portioning, thorough menu testing for customer acceptance and other operator measures will help reduce this waste, but ultimately it comes down to the guest deciding how much food goes into the garbage.

Packaging Waste. Packaging waste includes takeout containers, single-use cups, plastic bottles, disposable utensils, napkins and portion-controlled condiments, among other items. These items cost operators a lot of money, often are unnecessary for guests and rarely get recycled or composted.

As foodservice operators attack each of the above priorities, they will confront a range of confusing questions. For example, is it better to focus on composting pre-consumer food waste or donating the food? With post-consumer food waste, should one use a pulper, a digester, or a commercial composting facility? With packaging, does it make more sense to offer reusable plastic cups or compostable disposable cups?

To answer these questions, foodservice operators should refer to the waste management hierarchy, a pyramid that ranks waste management strategies in order of priority. Using this tool, operators can map options against the hierarchy and determine priority. For example, source reduction of pre-consumer food waste is always more important than either food donation or composting. With packaging, it is almost always better to offer reusable cups versus any compostable disposable option.

While the hierarchy can help prioritize, sometimes there are competing objectives which are not easily reconciled. Is your top goal to reduce costs? Waste less water? Reduce greenhouse gas emissions? Avoid using nonrenewable resources? Patronize local manufacturers? Operators often can find their way through confusing situations by listing and ranking their organizational goals.

For example, an operator might be struggling with the question of whether to purchase a compostable disposable cup if there is no way for the operation to compost that item. If the primary goal is to avoid buying products made from nonrenewable resources, it may not matter that the compostable cup will not be composted. The operator will have met the primary objective by purchasing the compostable cup even if it goes to landfill.

As foodservice operators explore waste management topics, they will encounter many of these trade-offs. It's not reasonable to expect easy answers in situations with so many variables. But it is possible to make clear, straightforward decisions once you know what you want to achieve.

There are several new third-party sustainability ratings systems available that identify waste management best practices. Even if an operator has no interest in pursuing a certification, [he or she] can use one of these standards as a roadmap to setting opportunities and goals.

The first nationally recognized standard is the Green Seal GS-46 Environmental Standard for Restaurants and Foodservices. It provides a detailed framework for waste management that will apply in whole or in part to most operations. Other standards that offer content relevant to specialized foodservices include the Green Guide for Health Care, the AASHE [Association for the Advancement of Sustainability in Higher Education] STARS system for colleges and universities and the APEX [Accepted Practices Exchange] standards for catering and convention centers. Each standard offers downloadable summaries, checklists and background information.

Tracking Waste Minimizes Waste

Foodservice operators will never avoid all waste, but they should prepare to strive for "zero waste." This means not putting any waste, especially food, in landfills. Foodservice operators can achieve zero waste through a combination of source reduction and waste diversion via food recovery, composting or recycling. Source reduction, which is perched at the very top of the waste management hierarchy, offers the highest cost-savings potential and dramatically better environmental outcomes than diversion.

Foodservice operators occasionally claim they have a zero waste operation if they compost or recycle pre- and post-consumer waste even if they lack focus on source reduction.

Composting has received considerable attention in recent years despite the fact that it ranks near the bottom of the waste management hierarchy. While composting is vastly preferable to landfill disposal, it should not be viewed as the singular antidote to food waste. A zero waste operation should focus heavily on source reduction and consider diversion a secondary option.

As the industry focuses more on source reduction, there also will be less tolerance for imprecise claims about waste reduction. Everyone wants to claim they are reducing waste, but this assertion is only true if you are preventing or minimizing waste at the source. Composting and food donation represent waste diversion tactics. In such cases, waste is diverted from a landfill for a higher and better use, but it has not been reduced.

Everyone wants to claim they are reducing waste, but this assertion is only true if you are preventing or minimizing waste at the source.

The only way to "see" source reduction is to track waste and regularly review the data. Tracking represents the return of a historical practice with deep roots. It was once common for chefs to stand by their garbage cans to monitor inflows and use logbooks to record waste. Time constraints forced these practices to the margin. But it's now important enough to revive even if it takes a little extra work. Also, new technology advances in food waste tracking make it feasible to automate what was once a manual process.

By measuring waste continuously, or at least frequently, operators establish a waste baseline and can measure progress over time. This data allows operators to break down the waste problem into subcomponents and set goals targeting specific areas and items.

With a feedback loop based on waste data, foodservice operators can raise staff awareness, obtain an edge through diagnostic information and create accountability where none previously existed. Once an operator meters waste, the process will begin to drive the systemic and behavioral changes necessary to minimize waste. Source reduction and tracking are two sides of the same coin.

The U.S. Environmental Protection Agency recently released a new version of its food waste calculator, an easy spreadsheet-based tool that helps foodservice operators predict waste reduction outcomes based on specific strategies. It also estimates environmental improvements and cost savings.

After launching an initiative and running it for several months, operators should evaluate actual savings. Start by using your waste tracking data collected in paper logbooks, a spreadsheet, or automated tracking systems to calculate food cost savings due to pre-consumer waste reduction. Then use your garbage bills to calculate disposal cost changes for both pre- and post-consumer food waste. Add the savings together and monitor changes monthly.

Compostable disposables have a prominent place in the current discussion about waste management. However, source reduction of disposable waste is still a much better solution than compostables if you have on-site diners and warewashing capabilities. By making every effort to encourage customers to take reusables, operators reduce waste and its impact on the environment.

As a first step, operators should require all foodservice workers eating on-site to use reusable ware. Then make disposables scarcer for regular guests and consider a surcharge.

New Waste Disposal Technologies

Even with extensive efforts to source reduce, there will be waste and it should be diverted away from landfills. Composting is one of the most common and effective diversion strategies, but many regions lack access to commercial composting facilities for food waste. While some operators may compost on-site, this is not a practical solution for most facilities. Commercial composting facilities offer great value because they master the technical nuances of composting and market the end product effectively. More operators will find themselves looking for commercial composting alternatives in 2010, and it's important they communicate this need to their municipality and garbage hauler. As operator demand increases, there will be incentives for private enterprise to develop more commercial composting alternatives.

Grinding food waste in a garbage disposer and sending it to a municipal wastewater treatment plant is another landfill diversion strategy. Since food is comprised of 70 percent water, this is often feasible and offers the benefit of avoiding hauling costs and emissions. Many wastewater treatment plants digest food waste with other organic matter and turn it into methane gas in a sealed system used to generate energy. This energy helps lower costs at the treatment plant and the remaining biosolids after the digestion process may be used as fertilizer. In this example, a garbage disposer would place higher on the waste hierarchy than composting because its industrial use leads to energy generation.

Even with extensive efforts to source reduce, there will be waste and it should be diverted away from landfills.

However, this solution may not be available or appropriate for all operators. Garbage disposers are not allowed in some jurisdictions. Not all wastewater treatment plants have the ability to turn food waste into energy and some treatment facilities are overloaded and don't want food waste. Critics argue that some disposers use too much water and that post-digestion biosolids may include contaminants. Still others worry about fats, oils and greases (FOG) in the sewer system, though research shows food waste rarely causes FOG build-ups.

Garbage disposers may be greener than people expect, but it depends on municipal regulations and infrastructure.

On-site food waste processing may be a good alternative if an operator lacks a commercial composting solution and does not want to dispose of food waste through a garbage disposer. There are several options:

In-vessel composting. Effective if an operator possesses the labor, space and technical know-how.

On-site aerobic digesters. These systems use enzyme-producing microbes, which digest food waste into nutrient-rich water effluent within hours. It's important to understand the digestion process and discuss it with the municipal sewage authority to ensure the digester effluent will be accepted.

Waste dehydrators. This solution extracts and evaporates water, reducing weight and volume of food waste and leaving a soil amendment as a by-product that is not compost.

Managing waste efficiently represents a chance to improve the bottom line while making a meaningful difference environmentally.

Waste Management of the Future

Here are a few trends on the horizon:

Customers Demand More Information. Customers have been clamoring to understand their food better in recent years: Where did it come from? Who grew it? Is it safe? These customers expect transparency around food, an attitude that will expand beyond food sourcing into the waste arena. Some customers now ask whether a restaurant composts its food waste and reuses its oil for biodiesel. Expect more questions and expectations of transparency and responsibility around waste handling in the future.

Regulations Exclude Food Waste from Landfills. More municipalities will strive to eliminate organics from landfills due to their greenhouse gas emissions. These regulators will create new requirements that may effectively prevent food waste from going to many landfills, forcing operators to develop more diversion alternatives.

Regulations Prevent Use of Non-Compostable and Nonrecyclable Disposables. Following Seattle's lead regulators across the country may prohibit non-compostable and nonrecyclable disposable packaging.

Waste to Energy Plants. Food waste can be converted to high-value energy by digesting waste and creating methane. Expect to see new digestion plants to digest food waste directly (not from the wastewater system) on a commercial scale to produce energy.

Learning to succeed on the new frontier of waste management may frustrate operators and test their patience. The payoff will be large enough to justify the investment. Managing waste efficiently represents a chance to improve the bottom line while making a meaningful difference environmentally.

In Spain, Garbage Management Is Improved

Tito Drago

In this viewpoint Tito Drago, a journalist and consultant specializing in international relations, discusses Spain's increasingly green methods of dealing with trash. Spain's green-friendly measures include the adoption of a green tax in Madrid, a proposed sustainable development bill, and countless waste reduction and recycling initiatives. The viewpoint focuses on automatic underground waste collection systems as especially noteworthy. Still, asserts Drago, the ultimate destination of waste has yet to be fully addressed.

As you read, consider the following questions:

1. What is Madrid's proposed green tax, according to Drago?
2. According to the viewpoint, what are some of Spain's environmental initiatives?
3. What are some benefits of central waste stations, as cited by Drago?

The 60,000 tonnes of rubbish collected daily in Spain, equivalent to 1.3 kilos [approximately 2.9 lbs.] per person, is being managed by more green-friendly methods of recovery and treatment.

One such measure adopted by the community (province) of Madrid is a non-fiscal tariff—a charge made for purposes other than revenue—"that we could call a green tax," Javier Martín Fernández, a professor of financial and tax law at the Complutense University [of Madrid], told IPS [Inter Press Service].

The tariff is in line with the position of the government of socialist Prime Minister José Luis Rodríguez Zapatero, which introduced a sustainable development bill to parliament in September.

Parliamentary sources told IPS that the bill is likely to pass, although opposition parties may propose certain reforms.

The commission defined sustainable development as development that meets the needs of the present without compromising the ability of future generations to meet their own needs.

The government adopted the definition of sustainable development approved in 1988 by the World Commission on the Environment and Development, created by the United Nations in 1983.

The commission defined sustainable development as development that meets the needs of the present without compromising the ability of future generations to meet their own needs.

Zapatero's bill aims to promote competitiveness through research, development and innovation (R+D+i), with the goal of increasing the use of renewable energy by 20 percent by 2020, as well as reducing overall energy consumption by 20 percent.

Environmental Initiatives

Waste reduction and recycling play an important role in this strategy. In a 2008 study of 18 cities, the northeastern city of Pamplona was the most efficient at recycling, recovering 53 percent of glass, 69 percent of paper and cardboard and 28 percent of throwaway bottles and containers, and coming closest to fulfilling the national waste plan.

Two biogas plants that began to operate this year [2009] at the Valdemingómez refuse processing centre in Madrid are using organic waste to produce methane, which in turn is used to generate electricity or distributed for household use.

A facility for maintaining and servicing a fleet of 120 waste collecting vehicles, installed in 2004 in the Villaverde district of Madrid, features 120 square metres of solar panels providing heating and hot water.

Water used at the facility is recycled, and used for washing the garbage collection trucks, which run on compressed natural gas, cutting pollution by 80 percent compared to conventional diesel-fuelled vehicles.

Another initiative in Elche, a city in the Mediterranean coastal province of Valencia where garbage containers are being installed, is an exchange system for residents, who can deposit a full rubbish bin and collect an empty one, for their convenience.

Interest in automatic underground waste collection systems is increasing, and by the end of this year they are expected to be used in 55 areas in Spain, including neighbourhoods in the cities of Barcelona, Tarrasa, Vitoria, Burgos and Mollerusa, where they will be servicing over one million people.

Standing out among these is the system being built at Barcelona airport, which handles 35 million passengers a year.

Users of the automated system deposit their refuse into post-box style waste inlets, in the street or inside a building, which are accessible 24 hours a day. There are different waste inlets for each type of refuse (organic, paper, and so on).

Garbage is then transported at 60 kilometres [approximately 37 miles] per hour along underground pipes into containers at a central waste station, by strong air currents produced by fans. At the central station the air is filtered and clean air is returned to the atmosphere. The sorted waste is then sent on for recycling or further processing.

Among the advantages of this system is that refuse is not scattered around a rubbish container in the streets, and the nuisance of noisy, polluting waste collection vehicles coming by in the nighttime hours is avoided.

In Majadahonda, a Madrid district where the system is already operational, Juan Barrios, a local resident, told IPS that apart from convenience and saving time, the collection system has done away with the mess of litter and rubbish spread around the old containers.

The streets here are quite empty of rubbish, in contrast to other Madrid neighbourhoods and other Spanish cities.

An important issue that still causes problems and is under further investigation is the final destination of waste and the ultimate recycling of the separated materials.

The latest official report by the National Statistics Institute indicated that only 10 percent of the total waste produced in

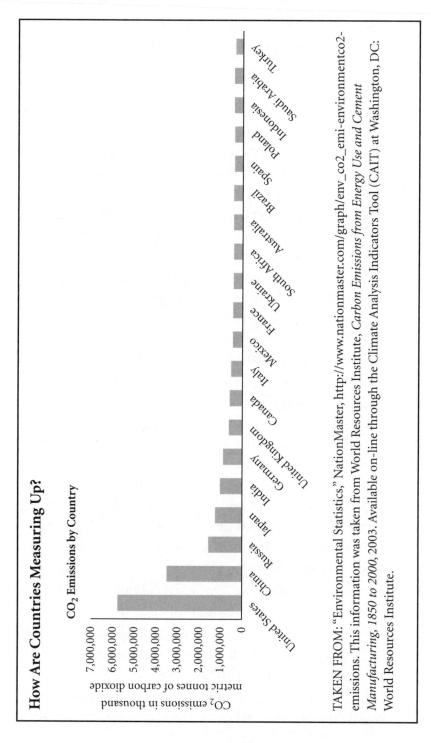

How Are Countries Measuring Up?

CO$_2$ Emissions by Country

CO$_2$ emissions in thousand metric tonnes of carbon dioxide

7,000,000
6,000,000
5,000,000
4,000,000
3,000,000
2,000,000
1,000,000
0

United States
China
Russia
Japan
India
Germany
United Kingdom
Canada
Italy
Mexico
France
Ukraine
South Africa
Australia
Brazil
Spain
Poland
Indonesia
Saudi Arabia
Turkey

TAKEN FROM: "Environmental Statistics," NationMaster, http://www.nationmaster.com/graph/env_co2_emi-environmentco2-emissions. This information was taken from World Resources Institute, *Carbon Emissions from Energy Use and Cement Manufacturing, 1850 to 2000,* 2003. Available on-line through the Climate Analysis Indicators Tool (CAIT) at Washington, DC: World Resources Institute.

Spain is sorted prior to collection. Of that proportion, one-quarter was glass, 10 percent was paper and cardboard, and the rest mixed waste.

An important issue that still causes problems and is under further investigation is the final destination of waste and the ultimate recycling of the separated materials.

The environmental activist group Greenpeace complained that a large part of collected refuse is wasted because sorting is done poorly or not at all, and the recovery of organic waste in particular is neglected.

The Spanish government's national waste plan calls for local governments to provide one street container for glass and one for paper and cardboard for every 500 people, and one for plastic bottles and containers for every 300 people, by 2015. This is already being done in about 20 cities.

An increasingly popular trend is for people who have a yard, vegetable patch or larger plot of land to recycle their organic waste into compost, to use as fertiliser.

Meanwhile, a state coordinating committee against the incineration of refuse by cement plants was formed on Oct. 10 [2009].

The committee claims that incineration is the most dangerous and unsustainable method of treating waste, because rather than eliminating, it spreads and scatters it, generating pollution and toxic emissions—a position that Greenpeace firmly supports.

In Canada, the Package Waste Problem Is Slowly Changing

Moira Welsh and Christopher Hume

In this viewpoint, Toronto Star *staff reporters Moira Welsh and Christopher Hume discuss the absolute necessity to cut back on product packaging, including products on the shelf, disposable coffee cups, and bottled soda and water. Although change is happening slowly, say Welsh and Hume, it is happening. The reporters argue that eventually society will look back at this time of extraordinary waste and see it for what it is, similar to the way society now views the dangers of drunk driving and smoking while pregnant.*

As you read, consider the following questions:

1. What examples of Ontario's extreme waste problem do the authors provide to argue that change is needed now?
2. What is the hierarchy of the Three Rs and why is the order important?
3. How are oceans "the great predictors of environmental change"?

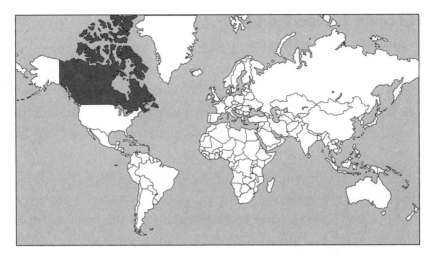

Twenty years ago, mothers smoked while reading bedtime stories to their children.

Professionals hit happy hour after work and joked about their drunken car drive home.

Ontarians filled their garbage bags with pop cans, newspapers, plastic water bottles and whatever else they wanted to get rid of.

No more.

What seems unimaginable now was once ordinary behaviour. All this has changed—and, most would say, for the better.

But although change has begun, it is far from complete. Limited space in Ontario landfill sites is being rapidly consumed by waste packaging—the cardboard and plastic boxes that wrap themselves around tiny toys, the hundreds of millions of coffee cups and the plastic beverage bottles that did not make it to recycling bins.

Time is running out, environmentalists and others say, for consumers and businesses to change their wasteful ways.

"If we don't make change, it is going to catch up with us," said Pascal Murphy, a master's student in York University's environmental studies program.

Change Is Needed Now

Millions of plastic bottles, grocery bags and coffee cups end up on the streets, beaches and forests as litter. Some of that plastic enters the water stream and, over time, can be carried as far as the Atlantic Ocean. Marine life, such as the endangered leatherback sea turtle, mistake plastic bags and bottles for jellyfish and eat them. And so the litter that originated in a faraway city gets trapped in their digestive system, often leading to starvation.

But an emerging movement against waste packaging is slowly gaining ground in Ontario. Some predict years from now its polluting presence will be diminished, much like smoking and drunk driving.

Just listen to Geoff Rathbone, who chuckles as he recalls organizing his first blue box program two decades ago. "It was in Essex-Windsor," says the general manager of the City of Toronto's solid waste department, "and the reaction there was, 'How can you expect us to separate our newspapers from our garbage? This is insanity!'

"That response seems laughable now. Twenty years hence, a lot of the things we are doing today will seem the same."

Tell that to the purveyors and consumers of Tim Hortons' coffee cups. When a Rathbone-penned staff report suggested last fall [2008] that Toronto coffee shops replace disposable coffee cups with reusable mugs or a deposit-return system, the proposal prompted outrage. A simple attempt to remove garbage from landfills became a controversy of double-double proportions.

While tossing a plastic pop bottle in the garbage instead of recycling bin does not carry the gravitas—and criminal penalty—of a drinking and driving charge, there is a growing public awareness that when it comes to the environment, change is needed now. Consider:

- Ontario residents, institutions and industries produce 12.4 million tonnes of garbage a year, the equivalent weight of more than 80,000 fully loaded Boeing 707 jetliners.

- Only 3 million tonnes are diverted from landfill sites into recycled goods, with about 6 million tonnes ending up in Canadian dumps.

- Four million tonnes of waste is trucked annually from Ontario to Michigan, where the state government has made it clear it does not want to continue accepting it.

- Many of Ontario's landfills will reach capacity in roughly 20 years.

A Waste Generation Crisis

Much of the garbage dumped in landfills is packaging. Residential blue bins overflow with packaging.

North Americans have been only too happy to buy into the disposable culture of consumerism, demanding the convenience of bottled water, coffee-to-go and hamburgers in Styrofoam containers.

"We don't have a waste disposal crisis," said Anastasia Lintner of Ecojustice. "We have a waste generation crisis. . . . We are gluttons."

"What we really have to do is teach the hierarchy of the 'Three Rs'; we must reduce first, then reuse, and finally, recycle."

As important as recycling has been to the environment, the original Three Rs included reducing and reusing—concepts consumers and industry did not embrace.

"We have been completely drilled into thinking of recycling as the solution to this problem of packaging," says

Heather Marshall of the Toronto Environmental Alliance. "It is not. Recycling is the last thing you would do before you throw it away. What we really have to do is teach the hierarchy of the 'Three Rs'; we must reduce first, then reuse and, finally, recycle."

Pop bottles are a good example: Historically most soft drinks in Ontario were sold in reusable glass bottles. Starting in the 1970s, the beverage industry introduced plastic bottles and aluminum cans, claiming they were safer and more convenient for consumers. More packaging created more garbage. Waste management became a top priority for governments.

In the 1970s, the environment ministry created new regulations requiring the phaseout of disposable bottles. Industry fought back, and an informal agreement was reached that required at least 75 per cent of bottled drinks to be sold in refillable containers, according to a paper by the Canadian Institute for Environmental Law and Policy. But government couldn't enforce it and today, almost all water and soft drinks are sold in disposable containers.

By the 1980s, disposable bottles proliferated, clogging landfills. The environment ministry responded with regulations that forced the soft drink industry to sell roughly 40 per cent of its products in refillable bottles, but those rules, according to waste consultant Clarissa Morawski, were never enforced.

"Most of the time voluntary initiatives fail," Morawski said. Strong laws create a level playing field and force change upon those who don't want to adapt, she says. Morawski cites Germany, which spent years in court fighting to establish government's right to force the use of refillable soft drink bottles.

Despite ignoring its own refillable bottle regulations, Morawski said Ontario's plan, called Toward A Zero Waste Future, represents a radical shift in environmental policy. Several changes have already been made, including the requirement that tire manufacturers pay for their disposal. The environ-

Primitive Trash

All human beings generate garbage. The quantity produced is exacerbated by civilization and urbanization. As humanity slowly advanced from hunters and gatherers to farmers and artisans, progress was marked by the accumulation of possessions. The character of acquired personal property identified the eras—Stone Age, Bronze Age, Iron Age. The discarding or abandonment of this property has helped tell the history of early man. When archaeologists excavate the dwellings of primitive people on any continent, they search first for the hearths and rubbish piles of the occupants. From this debris—broken tools, utensils, and weapons, gnawed and roasted bones, pottery shards, kernels of grain—and from the preserved remains of the inhabitants themselves, students of antiquity are able to determine the life, diet, and social order of our early ancestors. Had primitive man left behind only biodegradable trash, archaeologists would face a more challenging task.

Judd H. Alexander, In Defense of Garbage.
Westport, CT: Praeger Publishers, 1993.

ment ministry is working on its plan for legislative change, focusing on extended producer responsibility (EPR), which would require a manufacturer to pay the full cost of its product, including disposal.

The Environmental and Financial Cost of Excessive Packaging

It is also widely expected that the government plan will require industry to cover 100 per cent of the blue box program, which has a net annual cost of roughly $155 million. "We all need to recognize that EPR is here to stay," Ontario Environment Minister John Gerretsen told the annual meeting of Waste Diversion Ontario this month [April 2009].

Take Wal-Mart for example: The world's largest retailer is taking a leading role in reducing packaging of the products it sells.

It started in Canada last year by forcing laundry detergent companies to use concentrated products. Wal-Mart Canada spokesperson Karin Campbell says the company plans to require all suppliers to reduce packaging if they wish to remain in the stores. She estimates that 92 per cent of Wal-Mart's environmental footprint comes from packaging and this program is expected to reduce that by 5 per cent. That may not sound like much, but given the volume of the firm's sales—1 million customers a day—the impact would be significant: It will save 2.7 million kilograms of plastic resin, 3.6 million kilograms of cardboard and remove 1,200 delivery trucks from the roads over a three-year period, Campbell said.

Coca-Cola has decided to use lighter materials in its bottles and cans. But as Rathbone and others point out, volume—not weight—is what matters. "Our landfills will not be full because they're too heavy; they will be full when they reach their capacity," he says.

The movement against packaging has begun, albeit slowly.

The oceans are the great predictors of environmental change, and it is the Atlantic, off the coast of Nova Scotia, where Dalhousie University scientist Mike James studies the endangered leatherback sea turtle. The enormous turtles feed where ocean currents merge, pulling in their favoured food, jellyfish—and a massive field of plastic bottles and bags, chairs, balloons and beach balls from around the world.

The plastics are found in the bodies of dead albatross, porpoises, turtles and other marine life that confuse them for food. In the Pacific [Ocean], powerful currents pull the litter into seemingly endless piles of floating plastic, named the Plastic Killing Fields by researchers who study their impact on marine life.

The movement against packaging has begun, albeit slowly. Governments, especially Toronto's, will force grocery stores to charge a nickel for each plastic bag by June 1 [2009]. And Toronto has started to charge residents for the amount of garbage they produce.

But more importantly, these fees force people to question why industry can use excessive packaging that must then be paid for by residents. Financial incentives such as garbage fees play a huge role in behavior modification.

"It's like potty training," says Morawski. "Parents use incentives to train their children; if you go to the potty, you get a sticker. Proper waste diversion by citizens is very similar. It may be really hard to train a 2-year-old, but once they get it, they'll never go back. When it comes to garbage, we're the same."

Periodical Bibliography

The following articles have been selected to supplement the diverse views presented in this chapter.

Jessica Ablamsky   "For Our Planet & Our Pockets: Package of New Recycling Bills Would Help Environment, Save $$," *Queens Tribune* (New York), April 22, 2010.

BBC News   "New 'World Class' Recycling Plant," February 9, 2009. www.bbc.co.uk.

Fiona Cohen   "Next Garbage Mountain to Climb: Seattle Takes on Fast Food in July," *Seattle Post-Intelligencer*, April 20, 2010.

Penny Coles   "Message Is Clear: We Must Step Up Our Recycling," *Niagara Advance* (Ontario), April 22, 2010.

Marla Dickerson   "Tokyo's Goal: Be the Greenest," *Los Angeles Times*, April 23, 2010.

Rana Foroohor   "The Real Green Revolution," *Newsweek*, April 2, 2010.

Jenny Fyall   "Green Power Revolution to Create 500 Jobs a Month," *Scotsman*, March 23, 2010.

Greenpeace   "Victory! New Greener Computer Released in India," February 4, 2010. www.greenpeace.org.

Kathy Marks   "The Australian Town That Kicked the Bottle," *Independent* (UK), September 28, 2009.

Patt Morrison   "Dump the Foam," *Los Angeles Times*, August 16, 2007.

Denise Ngo   "Dustbot Comes When You Call It, to Pick Up Your Garbage and Take It Away," *Popular Science*, April 22, 2010.

Alternative Solutions to the Garbage and Recycling Dilemma

American Architect Turns Trash into Homes

Laura Sevier

In this viewpoint, Ecologist *deputy editor Laura Sevier celebrates Michael Reynolds as an environmental innovator. Dubbed the "Garbage Warrior," Reynolds designed the "Earthship," a self-sufficient home made out of recycled and natural materials. Reynolds—a trained architect who lost his architect's license for not following the rules—has built Earthships all over the globe, but not without encountering obstacles. Ironically, according to Reynolds, building the technically innovative homes has been easy, but dealing with bureaucracy has been beyond challenging.*

As you read, consider the following questions:

1. How are Reynolds's Earthships self-sufficient, according to the viewpoint?
2. What has been Reynolds's biggest challenge in getting Earthships built?
3. According to Sevier, what kinds of amenities do Earthships have?

Q uestion: What do you think of when you see a pile of old beer cans, bottles or car tyres? For most of us the answer is likely to be: a load of rubbish. Not everyone, however, sees it this way.

Laura Sevier, "Case Study: Building Sustainable Houses from Rubbish," *The Ecologist* (UK), June 19, 2009. Reproduced by permission. www.theecologist.org.

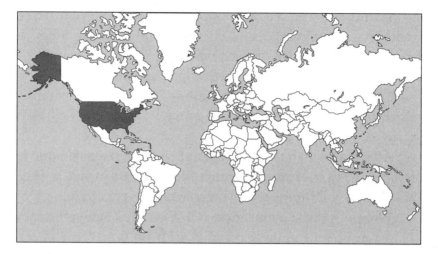

American architect Michael Reynolds considers tyres, bottles and cans 'natural resources'. Take tyres, he excitedly explains to me on the phone from his home in New Mexico— 'you can get them anywhere on the planet. In cities you have tyre stores that have to pay to get rid of old ones. In underdeveloped areas they're lying all over the place. Nothing good is really being done with them.'

Reynolds has found a way to turn garbage into what he describes as 'gold'—housing gold.

Since the 1970s he has been designing and building 'Earthships'—sustainable, self-sufficient homes that can be built from recycled and natural materials.

Beautiful, Sturdy and Efficient

You'd think that being built from unwanted garbage they'd be ugly, collapsible and makeshift. Yet these dome-shaped dwellings, which look more like spaceships than housing as we know it, have been described as 'magical', 'beautiful'—'the eighth wonder of the world' even. Plus, they are sturdy enough to withstand earthquakes measuring force nine on the Richter scale.

Reynolds built the first one in the New Mexico desert more than 30 years ago, and it's still standing strong today. In the small community of Taos where he still lives, he and his crew have constructed 60 Earthships over the years. They've had requests to build them around the world. Currently, Earthships are in use in almost every US state, as well as in many countries in Europe.

After more than three decades of refining the technique he says he is just 'starting to scratch the surface of what is available in this gold mine that we're starting to penetrate'.

What's valuable about these houses is their self-sufficiency. They can operate entirely off-grid, with no power, gas or water lines coming in and no sewage lines going out. Yet they still manage to keep their inhabitants warm.

'It's −18°C [Celcius] [0°Fahrenheit] outside when I wake up,' says Reynolds. 'Inside, the temperature is 21°C [70°F].'

It's all down to the design. The basic building blocks of an Earthship are earth-filled car tyres, using the concept of thermal mass both to cool and heat the buildings. On sunny days the sun soaks into the building and the mass holds the heat.

'What these kinds of houses are doing is taking every aspect of your life and putting it into your own hands.'

Internal, non-load-bearing walls are made out of mud or cement, with cans or bottles set like bricks. Earthships also make use of solar and wind electricity, contained sewage treatment and water-harvesting.

'What these kinds of houses are doing is taking every aspect of your life and putting it into your own hands,' says Reynolds. 'A family of four could totally survive here without having to go to the store.' Earthships even have internal space designed for growing food with drip-irrigation systems.

So what's it actually like to live in one? 'It's an empowering experience,' he assures me. 'It puts you in direct contact with sources—energy, water, heat. It makes you more able to take care of yourself. You're not so vulnerable.'

What's more, Earthships are relatively easy to build. Reynolds says the technology is 'graduate-school stuff. It's easy. It's there for the taking.'

In the realm of radically sustainable housing he is certainly a visionary. Earthships tick many eco-friendly boxes. Constructive use of rubbish: tick. Self sufficiency: tick. Suited to a post-oil world: tick.

Garbage Warrior

A 2007 documentary, *Garbage Warrior*, directed by Oliver Hodge, celebrated Reynolds's work and charted his struggle to get the houses built. It was, says Reynolds, 'a long and treacherous process'.

'The problem is all the bureaucratic, legal codes and regulations that are out there,' he explains. 'People are recognising that all over the developed world we have rules and laws in place to "protect" people, and this is holding people back from evolving. We need to evolve radically in how we build things.'

In the documentary, Reynolds comes across as a man on a mission. He sees his sustainable homes both as a solution and a 'direction for humanity'. Getting them built has meant 'breaking laws left, right and centre'.

Although a conventionally trained architect, he has always been a rebel: 'Everything I've ever done has been radical'. As a result of violating regulations he lost both his state and national architect's licences in the late 1990s. Everything he was doing fell outside what was considered 'legal construction'.

Later, the Earthship settlements were ruled illegally convened in breach of planning law. Job sites were shut down and building came to a grinding halt. Reynolds realised the only way to get things going again was to play by the rules, which meant making the settlement a legal subdivision, a process he describes as 'endless horseshit'. Inspections, lever-arch files of paperwork, archeologists, engineers, diagrams and drawings 'that nobody ever uses', all at a cost of thousands of dollars.

It took seven years to get the development completely open again, in 2004. Even so, he lost the right to experiment and create new buildings and innovations. There was no evolution, no scope to make mistakes.

What Reynolds wanted was a test site, with no holds barred. As he points out, 'They allow it for bombs, cars and aeroplanes—why not houses?' He realised that what was needed was a change in law to allow for easier testing of sustainable housing. 'Sometimes to fight the system you have to get in it and be part of the system,' he says.

It took him three-and-a-half years to write one law (the 'sustainable building test site' law), get it accepted in New Mexico and get the governors to sign. In 2007 his test site was finally approved by the state legislature.

Whereas in the US he had to beg on hands and knees to build, in other parts of the world Earthships have been welcomed with open arms. This was particularly marked in 2005 when Reynolds and his team were invited to one of the tsunami-hit Andaman Islands [territory of India].

There he introduced the concept of the low-tech shelter made from local materials and with the ability to withstand a force-nine earthquake, and showed them how to build an Earthship. 'They wholeheartedly jumped on the idea,' he says. 'There were no barriers. When there's an absolute breakdown of everything then new ideas are clutched like they could be lifesavers.'

Ironically, when the US board of architects heard about his work it invited him to reapply for his architect's licence.

The Next Step

Reynolds prefers to think of what he does as 'biotecture', a word he came up with 10 years ago to define a profession based on architecture, biology and physics. He points out that, over the years, the architectural establishment has viewed him as an idiot, incompetent, insane, a dreamer and even a crook. 'I scared a lot of people. I was building out of garbage. People's perceptions of it are changing, though. They're now seeing that it's a good material.'

He admits that in the early days there were 'f----ups'. There was the case of a writer who stayed in one of the Earthships and his typewriter melted. Sometimes the houses were too hot or leaked. 'I'm just glad I didn't kill anybody,' Reynolds says. As he's keen to emphasise, however, 'it's experimental. Some things don't work. Some things could be better.'

So what needs to happen next? He doesn't have faith in the legal process. Even though he got his law through in New Mexico, for it to appear in every state and county would take many more years of 'legislative bullshit', and as he says, 'we don't have that kind of time.'

'We know that in the future we're rendering this planet damn near uninhabitable.'

At the time of writing he was planning a talk at the UN [United Nations] in June [2009], about invoking martial law to apply the Sustainable Sites Act [Executive Order 13423, 2007] on a wider scale. 'Yes, there would be a few mistakes here and there, but it's way less damaging than this slow evolution. We're not keeping up.'

The Earthship model could potentially be rolled out on a larger scale. Reynolds wants to go to every city, constructing a building there to make it an educational facility.

'It's not just a shelter,' he says. 'You're building a machine that heats and cools, contains and treats its own sewage. It requires an education. So first you provide the prototype that they can replicate.'

The newest Earthship has a flat-screen TV and high-speed Internet connection. He says it's what people want and that it shows you don't have to live in a hut. The buildings have all amenities, such as hot showers and baths.

Do they work in other climates beyond New Mexico? 'Yes, but in severe areas like the Sahara Desert and the North and South poles they work to the extent of reducing the amount of fossil fuel.' Different climates suit different shapes—a building in Europe could be made to look very conventional, for example. 'But really, to hell with what it looks like: it's how it performs that matters.'

As Reynolds points out, 'We're running out of oil. We know that in the future we're rendering this planet damn near uninhabitable. So as we move towards that we're trying to devise a method of living that allows people to take care of themselves.'

In the Philippines, Residents Turn Trash into Useful Products

Ana Puod

In this viewpoint, journalist Ana Puod highlights communities in the Philippines that are finding innovative ways to turn waste into useful products. When one community had to clear countless water lilies after a devastating flood, residents turned the aquatic plants into useful goods such as handbags and slippers. In another Filipino community, residents built a sustainable business out of discarded juice pouches. Puod's viewpoint makes clear that environmentalism is beneficial to both the environment and the businessperson. Ana Puod is a writer for Inter Press Service news agency and is a member of the International Federation of Environmental Journalists.

As you read, consider the following questions:

1. According to Puod, what is the purpose of the Water Lily Livelihood Project?
2. Who are some big customers of the KILUS Foundation, according to the viewpoint?
3. How many doy packs has KILUS recycled into commercial items?

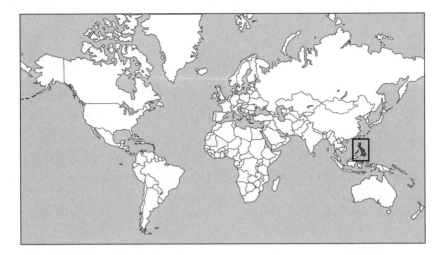

Days after the New Year's Eve revelry dies down, expect colorful lanterns or wreaths to remain hanging on the windows of many Filipino homes—part of a tradition in this Southeast Asian country known to have the longest Yuletide celebration in the world.

In Barangay (translated as 'village') Lower Bicutan, in Taguig City, located 15 kilometres [about 9 miles] east of Manila, the ubiquitous holiday decorations are a testament to a never-say-die spirit and ingenuity. They are mostly fashioned out of water lilies that clog the town's drainage system instead of the conventional bamboo sticks, Japanese and crepe paper that have come to be associated with the iconic symbol of the Filipino Christmas.

A Tragedy Leads to Innovation

Taguig City outlines Laguna de Bay, one of the biggest freshwater lakes in Asia and the Philippines' largest inland body of water. Water lilies are known to thrive in such bodies of water, growing to a height of 40 inches and multiplying fast. Thus they can easily displace local aquatic plants and adversely affect water quality and flow.

When Typhoon Ketsana unleashed its wrath in late September [2009], the village of approximately 44,000 residents found itself submerged in water as did other parts of the city. "We are so used to flooding, but 'Ondoy' (local name of the typhoon) was different," says resident Lolita Remillo, adding that many of her "kababayan (fellowmen) died." Water lilies were deemed among the culprits behind Taguig's submergence in floodwater.

But city councilor Gigi de Mesa sees a bright side to this otherwise tragic event. "The flooding even pushed the water lily nearer to the shore. This even made it easier for us to collect water lilies."

"We are not only creating jobs but helping the environment as well."

Just a month before Ketsana hit the country, the city government launched the Water Lily Livelihood Project, which aimed to provide a source of income for the communities in the city, particularly women, while clearing Laguna de Bay of water lilies. "The primary purpose of the project is to generate livelihood among the people of Taguig City, especially women," says Kaye Tinga, wife of city mayor Fred Tinga.

The project involves collecting the nuisance aquatic plants and turning them into useful products. "We are not only creating jobs but helping the environment as well," reasons de Mesa, one of the organisers of the project that has turned into a cooperative.

Through the training spearheaded by Kaye Tinga, community members learned how to weave products like bags, place mats, slippers and Christmas decors like lanterns and wreaths out of water lilies. Some 200 people were initially trained, followed by another batch of 800, who were then taught about various aspects of the livelihood project.

The recycling process is straightforward. Upon harvest, the plants are dried under the sun and then cured and dyed before they are woven into craft articles. A certain level of inventory of processed water lilies is maintained to ensure a steady supply of raw materials and enable the project proponents to determine the volume of orders that can be realistically accepted. Daily gross sales average 10,000 pesos (217 U.S. dollars). At the onset of this year's Christmas season, orders began to increase. This enabled the workers to earn an average of 2,000 to 3,000 pesos (44 to 65 dollars) each a week.

From Garbage to Handbag

Taguig City is not alone in its efforts to make something useful out of otherwise environmental hazards. Not too far from Taguig is Pasig City—some 12 km [about 7.4 miles] east of Manila—which was similarly inundated by floodwaters at the height of Typhoon Ketsana.

A community-based multipurpose cooperative in Barangay Ugong, one of numerous villages comprising the city, collects and recycles used juice plastic pouches as part of its campaign to recycle non-biodegradable products into colorful handbags, slippers, cellular phone cases, umbrellas and other items.

"It started when we visited a dump site. We saw that they were burning rolls of doy packs from the factories," recounts Editha Santiago, founder of KILUS Foundation, which stands for Women United for the Nation's Progress. "We remembered our own collection of used doy packs [sealed plastic pouches designed to stand upright; often used for single-serving juice]. We thought we could come up with something. That kind of garbage should not be burned."

The foundation, which was organised in 1999 as an all-women group, approached several doy pack manufacturers asking them to buy its collection of used doy packs, but only one of them agreed. Big multinational companies turned it down.

"That's when we intensified our drive to collect doy packs, the packaging of which is colorful and sturdy, so we thought hard about what to make out of them," explains Santiago. Members of the foundation regularly visited nearby barangays or villages in the city, including funeral homes, churches and schools, to buy used juice packs for 20 centavos each (or less than 1 U.S. cent).

In 2000, KILUS launched its own line of doy bags.

When the project started, it sold only a few items, mostly to the members' families and friends. But word soon spread in nearby towns and cities about the ingenious recycled products. Soon KILUS was deluged with orders prompting it to expand its production to seven other villages within the city.

The cooperative's membership base has expanded to include entire families, including children. Around five percent of current members are males, says Santiago.

KILUS has been featured both in local and international media like BBC and CNN. Its products have graced international publications such as the U.S.'s *Teen Vogue*, Britain's the *Observer* and those in Japan.

The global campaign against climate change has generated greater interest in its products, particularly abroad. Bulk orders are from Europe and Japan, with more regular orders coming in from the United States. The largest U.S. book retailer, Barnes & Noble, is its latest addition to its international clientele.

"Since last year we have made six shipments of 20-foot container (vans) to them (Barnes & Noble). I think they sell our tote bags at 16.95 U.S. dollars each," says Santiago.

In the aftermath of typhoons Ketsana and Parma, says Santiago, they got even more orders from their foreign clients.

Practical Recycling

In the 1990s, Ahmed Khan's company in Bangalore, India, churned out hundreds of thousands of plastic bags and other packaging material each month. . . . Now, he is in the business of scouring the city's landfills and trash cans to reclaim some of that waste. . . .

[He] is trying to solve two of the biggest problems in India: battered roads and overflowing landfills. His solution: streets made with recycled plastic.

[His company] has built more than . . . 745 miles of roads using 3,500 tons of plastic waste.

Mridu Khullar,
"Plastic Roads Offer Greener Way to Travel in India."
New York Times, *November 14, 2009.*

Environmentalism Makes Good Business Sense

What started out as a small community undertaking is now a profitable cottage industry that has been a steady source of income for some 50,000 residents of Pasig.

Tears welling up in her eyes, Santiago says one worker was able to construct a toilet in her house using her earnings. KILUS members can generate as much as 8,000 pesos (174 dollars) monthly during peak seasons.

Clara Buctuan, another member, says she joined the cooperative to augment her husband's income as a tricycle driver. Her monthly earnings of 6,000 pesos (130 dollars) allow her to send their two children to school and help with other household expenses.

Joining the foundation helped her in other ways. "I gained self-confidence," she says. The self-proclaimed environmentalist adds that she also takes pride in being able to help the environment.

Tears welling up in her eyes, Santiago says one worker was able to construct a toilet in her house using her earnings.

Since it started, KILUS has recycled 90 tonnes of doy packs into commercial items, including bags.

The water lily lanterns still hanging on residential windows in Taguig and the doy fashion bags produced in Pasig are a constant reminder to their residents that there is money in trash. Sound environmental practices, they say, make good business sense.

In China and Beyond, Trash Is Turned into Art

PRNewswire-Asia

In the following viewpoint, PRNewswire-Asia reports on the results of the Touchmedia Eco-Art China 2010 competition. The purpose of the Eco-Art China campaign was to inspire people to rethink their attitudes toward garbage and use the principles of reduce, reuse, and recycle to turn "trash into art." Touchmedia used its in-taxi interactive touch screens to promote the Eco-Art China 2010 competition.

Touchmedia was founded in 2003, by its chairman, Micky Fung, to develop state-of-the-art touch screen media technology. It is the largest in-taxi interactive media company in China.

As you read, consider the following questions:

1. Who was the first place winner of the Eco-Art China 2010 competition, and what materials did he use?
2. Who is Louis Dussault, and what part did he play in the Eco-Art China 2010 competition?
3. What two companies, other than Touchmedia, are mentioned as contributors to the Eco-Art China 2010 competition, and what are their stated reasons for assisting the competition?

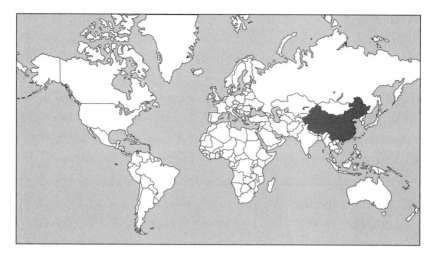

Shanghai, China, Sept. 7/PRNewswire-Asia/—Artworks made from trash were crowned at the Montreal Case Pavilion, Expo 2010 [Shanghai China] as winners of Touchmedia's Eco-Art China 2010 competition. Tan Lu from Sichuan won 1st place and a trip for two to Montreal with his work made of soda cans, cotton flannel, foam and cardboard. Mr. Michel Bissonnet, member of the executive committee for the City of Montreal, and Ray Lui, the honorary chairman of Touchmedia, presented the awards. The 1st and 2nd place winners will be exhibited at Montreal Case Pavilion until October 31st.

1st place winner Tan Lu, a 33-year-old hearing-impaired railway worker, spent 10 days working on a delicate and intricate cutting and engraving artwork called *Peony & Phoenix*. It was a piece he felt represented the spirit of his community, Mian Yang City, an area still rebuilding from the 2008 earthquake in Sichuan. "I hope my work can be exhibited at the Expo to be enjoyed by visitors from all over the world. Let them feel the passion and wisdom of Sichuan people in rebuilding their beautiful homes."

Lu will fly to Montreal and will officially be welcomed by the City of Montreal. Mr. Michel Bissonnet said, "The City of Montreal is delighted to welcome the Eco-Art China 2010 winner and shall be officially received by the mayor. He will also tour the Environmental Complex of Saint-Michel, the state-of-the-art case that Montreal is proudly presenting at the Expo 2010. Montreal is known worldwide as a vibrant, creative and sustainable city; that is why a partnership between Montreal and Eco-Art China 2010 was obvious! Montrealers appreciate that a better city means a better life, and this way of living is reflected in our daily actions and initiatives."

1st place winner Tan Lu ... [presented] a delicate and intricate cutting and engraving artwork called Peony & Phoenix *[that] he felt represented the spirit of his community, Mian Yang City, an area still rebuilding from the 2008 earthquake in Sichuan.*

For Mr. Louis Dussault, official representative for the City of Montreal to Expo 2010, "Eco-Art China is a great and creative initiative, the Montreal Case team and I are proud to be related to this project promoting eco-responsibility for everyone, and most of all to contribute to its success. We wish long life to Eco-Art China!"

Old, Young, East to West, Amateurs and Professionals: All Turning Trash into Treasure

Eco-Art China campaign aims to motivate the public to rethink their attitude towards garbage and discover the principles of reduce, reuse and recycle by turning 'trash into treasure'. A local green idea inspired by the 2010 world expo's Better City Better Life theme, and developed by Touchmedia, has helped to fuel global eco passion. With Touchmedia's in-taxi interactive touch screens as the key vehicle to promote the Eco-Art China 2010 campaign, passengers interacted directly with the screens to find out about the contest, request entry forms, learn about industry eco initiatives, download

Eco-Art digital wallpaper, view the top works and help decide the winner. In six weeks, 39,599 e-mail addresses were entered by taxi passengers requesting contest entry forms. After a panel of 10 judges from 5 countries shortlisted the top 4 works for public voting, taxi passengers cast about 90,000 votes in two weeks. The 3 1/2 month long campaign reached over 75 million people in Shanghai, Beijing, Guangzhou and Shenzhen. The response demonstrates an extremely high level of public interest in environmental protection combined with artistic creation at the local, domestic and global levels.

Contest participants ranged from 8 to 72 years of age from 13 Chinese cities plus France, Japan and Taiwan resulting in a variety of personal stories and unlimited inspiration.

Also winning 3rd place was a group of architects, designers and artists called YA + K, based in France, who submitted a mobile city kitchen made from recycled plastic, wood, metal, old gas cookers and sinks.

Two Shanghai artists, Yang Yan and Jun Wang, who won 2nd and 3rd prizes respectively in Eco-Art 2009 both collected 2nd prize honors for their 2010 works which used clay, wire mesh, wax, glass, paint, canvas, boxes, insulation and paint. Two eight-year-olds from Zhang Jia Gang, Hao Huang and Yibei Wang, claimed the third 2nd prize spot with their pair of birds pieced together from Tetra Pak milk boxes.

Claiming the five 3rd place spots included Tomiyo Yamada from Japan, known as Expo Granny, who entered her ukiyo-e (Japanese typical prints) of FUJI Mountain. Also winning 3rd place was a group of architects, designers and artists called YA + K, based in France, who submitted a mobile city kitchen made from recycled plastic, wood, metal, old gas cookers and sinks. Three other 3rd prize winners were from the Chinese cities of Jinghua, Guangzhou and Shanghai.

Multiplying the Eco Impact Through Collective Corporate Efforts

Micky Fung, founder and chairman of Touchmedia, said, "In addition to the huge response from the general public and the Shanghai Environmental Protection Bureau's involvement as official supporting body, many other companies including Skoda and Tetra Pak extended their support to the campaign. I hope that Eco-Art China becomes a catalyst to drive widespread participation and responsibility in protecting our environment through individual actions and industry initiatives."

"Encouraging more people to turn 'trash into treasure' mirrors our commitment of recycling post consumed cartons, which can be made into useful products such as the benches installed in the Expo park."

Said Carol Yang, vice president, Tetra Pak China, the world's leading food processing and packaging solutions company, "At Tetra Pak, we design our packages to be environmentally advantageous. The involvement with Eco-Art China falls into our agenda to continuously increase the public's awareness of environmental protection. Encouraging more people to turn 'trash into treasure' mirrors our commitment of recycling post consumed cartons, which can be made into useful products such as the benches installed in the Expo park."

Peter Miling, executive director of Skoda Sales & Marketing, Shanghai Volkswagen, expressed, "At the individual level, choosing fuel-efficient vehicles over normal vehicles is a significant factor in reducing collective CO_2 emissions; Green-Line uses Eco-Art China's platform to showcase the green GDP environmental idea we always pursue, which is the insistence on the green concept, design requirements on energy saving and the relentless pursuit of low- power, high-dynamic performance."

A British Entrepreneur Turns Waste into Fuel

Danny Fortson

In this viewpoint, British journalist Danny Fortson argues that Britain must work to move beyond its bad standing in the recycling world. To do so, it would be in the country's best interest to pay attention to what he calls "rubbish tycoons," businesspeople trying to make a profit on the world's mounting trash problem. Fortson focuses on one rubbish tycoon in particular, Philip Hall, whose company converts trash into fuel. Unfortunately, says Fortson, the United Kingdom is not paying enough attention.

As you read, consider the following questions:

1. How does Reclaim's Vantage Waste Processor work, according to Fortson?
2. From where are most of Reclaim Resources' customers?
3. According to the viewpoint, how much will Britain need to invest in order to cut its landfilling in half?

Yesterday, like every day, you produced 3 lbs. of rubbish. A third of it will be recycled, and some of it will be burnt. Most of it, though, will be tossed into a hole in the ground to rot away over several decades.

As it decays it will generate methane, a greenhouse gas 23 times more harmful than carbon dioxide, and leachate, a pu-

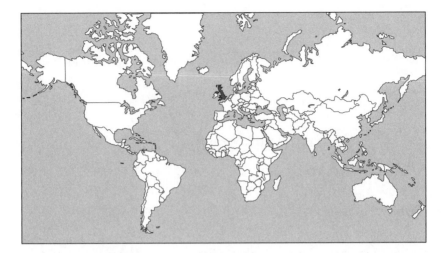

trid black liquid that must be pumped out of the ground to keep it from fouling the water table. Some material, such as plastics, will never break down fully.

The government is, belatedly, trying to change Britain's standing as among the worst recyclers in western Europe. It has imposed a swingeing landfill tax that is rising every year. The scramble to avoid it has led to a new generation of rubbish tycoons, all hoping to cash in on the move to waste less and recycle more.

One of them is Philip Hall. The 62-year-old serial entrepreneur has developed a technology that converts waste into bioethanol, a green alternative to petrol. His company, Reclaim Resources, built its first demonstration plant in Bournemouth [in England] last year [2009].

"We either set fire to our garbage or bury it. I thought, there has to be a better way."

The idea came to him in 2005, when an incinerating company asked his previous firm, X Technology, to fit its odour-control kit to its ovens.

Hall said: "We either set fire to our garbage or bury it. I thought, there has to be a better way." The result was Reclaim's Vantage Waste Processor, which blasts rubbish with high-pressure steam as it passes through a giant rotating cylinder. The process breaks down all organic material into fine fibres with high calorific value. The plastic and metal is removed and taken away for recycling.

The biological leftovers are converted into sugars through hydrolysis and acid treatment and then fed into large fermentation tanks. These break them down into fuel that can be blended for use in cars and aircraft or to feed the gas turbines of a power station.

Putting the Plan into Action

Turning the country's waste into a limitless source of biofuel sounds too good to be true—and so far that seems to be the view taken by Britain's councils and developers.

The company's handful of orders are all from foreign firms. "I have to say the UK [United Kingdom] has been pretty disappointing," said Hall. "The real interest is coming from the developing world—China, Malaysia, Russia. I imagine the first 30 plants will be built overseas before we have one running in England."

What is certain is that Britain needs to do better with its waste. We bury 58% of the 220m [million] tonnes of waste we produce every year. By 2013, landfilling must be cut to half of 1995 levels. If that level is not achieved, Britain will violate the EU [European Union] landfill directive and be subject to hefty fines.

To prod the industry into action, the government has raised landfill taxes and offered generous subsidies for waste-to-energy developers. AMA Research, an American consultancy, said Britain will have to invest £30 billion [approximately $45 million] to put the infrastructure into place.

Flexible Fuel Vehicles

Flexible fuel vehicles are those that run on ethanol or gasoline. The following automobile manufacturers design flexible fuel vehicles:

- Chrysler
- Ford/Lincoln/Mercury
- General Motors
- Isuzu
- Mazda
- Mercedes
- Nissan
- Toyota

Growth Energy,
"Flexible Fuel Vehicles," www.e85fuel.com.

Apart from Reclaim's demonstrator plant in Bournemouth it has made only one other unit and is near to completing a third in Latvia [a country in northern Europe], where labour costs are a fraction of those in Britain. Hall has sunk £3m [approximately $4.5 million] of his own money and cash from private investors into the company and is now trying to raise another £10m [approximately $15 million] to step up production.

Hall's is just one of a handful of waste-to-energy alternatives being developed. Anaerobic digestion, for example, uses giant steel tanks filled with microbes to break down organic waste. J Sainsbury, the supermarket group, is building several anaerobic digesters to get rid of date-expired food. The process takes 40 days.

Reclaim, on the other hand, takes only three days to start producing ethanol and then its plant can operate continuously.

A syndicate of underwriters has enough confidence in the technology to offer performance bonds covering loss of income in case the ethanol production is less than capacity. "As long as there is a continuous waste source," Hall said, "it's like a tap."

In Sweden, Alcohol and Human Waste Fuel Cars

David Wiles

David Wiles is editor of Sweden Today. *In this viewpoint, Wiles celebrates how Sweden is learning to become less dependent on oil. As part of a plan to become oil free by 2020, he reports, the Swedish government began using confiscated alcohol as well as human feces and animal carcasses to make biogas to fuel cars. In addition to being environmentally conscientious, using ethanol instead of oil is cheaper. Wiles notes that Sweden is further encouraging oil-free lifestyles by giving "green" cars free passes on toll roads and free parking in many cities.*

As you read, consider the following questions:

1. Why does Swedish customs confiscate so much alcohol, according to Wiles?
2. What is in the "stomach-churning mixture" used to make biogas, as explained in the viewpoint?
3. According to Wiles, what are the benefits of using biogas for fuel?

Swedes could soon be filling their cars with smuggled alcohol and animal remains. It is all part of a plan by the Swedish government to wean the country off oil within 15 years and thereby become the world's first oil-free country.

David Wiles, "The Road to Sweden's Oil-Free Future," Sweden.se, March 31, 2006. Reproduced by permission.

Sweden already gets most of its electricity from nuclear and hydroelectric power. Now it's turning its attention to transport, and petrol and diesel.

There are a number of alternative transport fuels in use today around Sweden, which is ranked the second most environmentally friendly country in the Environmental Performance Index.

From Booze to Fuel

The high price of alcohol in Swedish liquor stores results in a constant stream of day-trippers traveling to neighboring Germany and Denmark to stock up on cheap beer, wine and spirits. Last year [2005], under the "personal use" rule, Customs seized 55,000 liters of spirits, 294,000 liters of strong beer and 39,000 liters of wine.

Peter Nielsen is head of intelligence at Tullverket (Swedish Customs) in Malmö, south Sweden. "When I became a Customs officer in 1986 it was standard procedure to just pour these drinks down the sink," he says.

"But now there is this new environmental awareness. No one gains from pouring it away, not financially or environmentally. So we have gone from washing it down the sink to using an advanced plant for generating biogas and environmentally friendly fertilizers."

The one million bottles and cans seized annually by Tullverket are trucked to a warehouse where they are dumped into a crushing machine. The beverages are separated from their containers and blended with water to make the largest and probably worst-tasting cocktail imaginable. This is then taken by tanker to a plant in Linköping, about 200 km [approximately 124 miles] south of Stockholm, and turned into biofuel to power public buses, taxis, garbage trucks, private cars—even a train.

The biogas train, which has been running between Linköping and Västervik on the southeast coast for six months, has generated international interest and the technology behind it could soon be taken up by India.

Peter Undén is the marketing boss at Svensk Biogas, which produces, distributes and sells biogas for transportation in eastern Sweden. Each year the company takes 50,000 tons of a stomach-churning mixture of slaughterhouse waste, human waste and seized alcohol and turns it into clean-burning biogas.

He says that when the local food processing industry slaughters cows and other animals, it is left with blood, innards and other small pieces of superfluous meat. "Before, this just went to a landfill and would lay there and rot and create methane seepage," he says. "So it's a good thing to use this energy in a positive way."

This miracle of science, where waste products are turned into a fuel that produces only five per cent of petrol emissions, takes place in an anaerobic digester.

"When these waste materials reach our plant we mix them together, heat them to 70C [158°F] then put them into the anaerobic digesters," Undén explains. "The organic materials

Running on Booze

How did I first learn about alcohol's ability to run vehicles? I can still remember, as clear as a bell, talking about brewing beer (which was still illegal in 1974) with Doc Sweeney, one of my ecological biology professors at San Francisco State. He was infamous for telling students outrageous tall tales with a straight face just to see their reaction, or better yet, to see if he could get away with it.

He said to me, "That beer you're brewing could even run your car."

His deadpan expression was daring me. "You're lying." I said.

And, as any really excellent teacher would, he said, "Prove it."

So I went to the library, figuring this was going to be the needle in the haystack search of all time. Much to my surprise, I found more than 30 books from the early part of the 20th century. There was a whole hidden history of alcohol as a fuel that my friends and I had never known existed. Damn that Sweeney; he hooked me good.

David Blume,
Alcohol Can Be a Gas!
Fueling an Ethanol Revolution for the 21st Century.
Ed. Michael Winks. Santa Cruz, CA:
International Institute for Ecological Agriculture, 2007.

are broken down for 30 days and during that process biogas is produced. When the gas comes out, we clean it and sell it."

Undén says the benefits of using biogas for fuel are that it is renewable, carbon dioxide neutral and produced locally, thereby creating jobs and reducing transportation costs.

Life After Oil

Mattias Goldman of Gröna Bilister (the Swedish Association of Green Motorists) says there are other advantages for saying farewell to fossil fuels. "It's pure economics. If you run on ethanol you save about [Swedish krona] SEK 1.50 [.21¢] per 10 kilometers [approximately 6.2 miles] compared with petrol. When you run on biogas you can save up to SEK 5 [.70¢] per 10 kilometers [approximately 6.2 miles]."

Goldman points out that drivers of "green" cars don't have to pay the road tolls in Stockholm and park for free in many of Sweden's larger cities. "Plus company car drivers pay less car tax," he says. "It is not the Greenpeace activist but the company car driver that is making the market for green cars grow rapidly in Sweden."

With this level of engagement among the public, determination within the government and a fair dose of ingenuity, Sweden may yet prove that there is life after oil.

Today almost 40,000—or one per cent—of the four million cars on Swedish roads run on alternative fuels. Last year sales were up 168 per cent. By the end of the year green cars are expected to account for about 20 per cent of new car sales.

With this level of engagement among the public, determination within the government and a fair dose of ingenuity, Sweden may yet prove that there is life after oil.

In Space, Recycling Faces New Dilemmas

Jon Excell

Jon Excell is editor of the Engineer, *a magazine that reports on the latest developments and technology in engineering. In this viewpoint, he reports on the MELiSSA system (Micro-Ecological Life Support System Alternative), which might help humans to endure deep space exploration in the future. Currently in the pilot phase, MELiSSA is a five-chamber waste disposal system that generates food, oxygen, and water. Excell notes that such a system would be necessary for deep space exploration because of the problem of transporting heavy loads of water and oxygen into orbit. Although a full-scale MELiSSA system is years away, it offers hope for future space expeditions, he concludes.*

As you read, consider the following questions:

1. What is the difficulty involved with carrying vast amounts of water and oxygen into space, according to Excell?
2. How is MELiSSA's technology used on land, according to the viewpoint?
3. How is MELiSSA different from other similar systems, as explained by Excell?

A European-developed processing plant designed for recycling human waste could be at the heart of future manned space missions to Mars and beyond, the *Engineer* has learned.

Inaugurated earlier this month [June–July 2009] at Barcelona's Autonoma University, the so-called Melissa system (Micro-Ecological Life Support System Alternative) uses a suite of technologies largely borrowed from the process industry to recover food, water and oxygen from waste products, including faeces [feces], urine, and carbon dioxide.

Partly funded by the European Space Agency (ESA), the project could get around one of the fundamental stumbling blocks to a prolonged presence in space: the problem of transporting vast quantities of water and oxygen into orbit. Melissa coordinator, ESA's Dr Christophe Lasseur explained its potential: If we want to have a long duration presence in space, life-support consumables will be a very important issue. To stay alive you need 5kg [approximately 11 lbs.] per day per person of consumables—water, food, oxygen—if you have a crew of six on a 500-day mission you will reach tonnes very easily. He added that if you add nonessential but highly desirable products for washing to this mix the amount of mass you need to lift into orbit for longer trips rapidly becomes untenable.

Lasseur explained that the current pilot plant—the result of more than 20 years of research—is effectively an artificial ecosystem.

Based on a mixture of off-the-shelf systems and technology developed specifically for the project, the facility consists of five interconnected compartments. The first three compartments employ a number of techniques to progressively break down the waste.

In the first chamber—the liquefying compartment—a variety of bacteria are used to anaerobically transform urine, faeces and other waste to ammonium, volatile fatty acids and minerals. A complementary process oxidises the fibrous material in the waste. In the second compartment organic carbon is removed while in the third a process based on a fixed-bed reactor uses nitrosomas and nitrobacter bacteria to oxidise the ammonium to nitrites, then to nitrate. The products of these processes—CO_2, nitrate, and other minerals—are pumped into a fourth compartment where, along with sunlight, they can be used to grow algae or plants to generate food, oxygen and water.

The final and fifth chamber is where the crew lives, in the case of the Melissa project a group of 40 rats whose combined oxygen consumption is, said Lasseur, roughly equivalent to a single human being.

Closing the Loop

Currently, the compartments are being tested independently, but Lasseur hopes to connect them up and close the loop within the next couple of years. Once this happens the waste generated by the 'crew' will then be fed back into the first chamber and the benefits of the system will become ever more apparent. Lasseur added that according to simulations the current system will recycle around 70 per cent of the waste it generates. The longer-term aim however, is to have a 100 per cent efficient system.

While the incorporation of a full-scale Melissa system onto a spacecraft is some years away, Lasseur said that elements of the programme are already beginning to bear fruit. 'Today we already have technology that we can use coming from the Melissa research,' he said. Indeed, microbial detection systems developed as part of the project have already been used on the Automated Transfer Vehicle (ATV) used to supply the International Space Station. While closer to home water treatment systems developed through Melissa are currently used to process around 1.8 million cubic metres of water a day across Europe.

The project has also led to the development of two spin-off companies; Ipstar which is devoted to general technology

---

NASA Advances Water Recycling for Space Travel and Earth Use

Would Columbus have reached the New World if his ships could not carry enough water for their crews? Would Lewis and Clark have made it to the Pacific if they had no fresh water along the way?

The answer is probably no, because water is just as precious to explorers as it is to everyone on Earth. Water is one of the most crucial provisions astronauts need to live and work in space, whether orbiting Earth, working at a lunar base or traveling to Mars. That's why NASA [National Aeronautics and Space Administration] is following several different but complementary avenues at four agency centers to develop dependable ways of recycling water.

John Bluck and Dolores Beasley,
"NASA Advances Water Recycling for Space Travel and Earth Use,"
NASA (news release), November 12, 2004. www.nsa.gov.

---

transfer from the programme; and Ezcol, which is exploring the potential of a cholesterol lowering micro-organism used in Melissa.

Lasseur puts much of this success down to the multidisciplinary nature of the team: a wide-ranging alliance of engineers, biologists, and mathematicians drawn from across industry and academia. On a daily basis you will inevitably have some indirect return by bringing a large European community around the table, he commented.

Lasseur added that the system is very different from anything that has been attempted in the past and goes further, for instance, than recycling systems used on Mir [Russian space station] or the International Space Station (ISS) that purify water and recycle urine and exhaled carbon dioxide. 'Today on board the ISS they mainly recover the water condensate; around a month ago they brought a urine recycling machine, but there is nothing in terms of air and food,' he said. The chief difference, though, is that such systems are relatively piecemeal and employ stand-alone units that perform specific functions. Melissa is the only project that attempts to connect all of these systems together in a closed artificial ecosystem. The closest equivalent to Melissa is the CEEF (closed ecology experiment facility) in Aomori, Japan, which is employing a similar approach not for space applications but to monitor the possible effects on ecosystems of nuclear fallout.

When it does make this leap, the scientists on the Melissa programme will have achieved something of great significance: the technology necessary to sustain human life in the depths of space.

It's taken the Melissa project around 20 years to get to its current stage, and Lasseur said that it may be another 20 years before the technology finds its way onto flight hardware. When it does make this leap, the scientists on the Melissa programme will have achieved something of great significance: the technology necessary to sustain human life in the depths of space.

Periodical Bibliography

The following articles have been selected to supplement the diverse views presented in this chapter.

Jonah Bliss   "Four Stunning Works of Art Made from Re-cycled Trash," Geekosystem, April 22, 2010. www.geekosystem.com.

Hilary Dickinson   "Pay-As-You-Throw Initiated," *Beloit Daily News* (Beloit, Wisconsin), April 23, 2010.

Daniel Gross   "Trimming Waste: A Greener, Cheaper Way to Deal with Garbage," *Slate*, September 9, 2009.

Roger Highfield   "How a Rubbish Idea Could Save the Planet," *Telegraph* (UK), September 29, 2009.

Japan Today   "Bra Recycling—Newest Trend in Eco-Consciousness," July 17, 2009.

Chrissy Kadleck   "System Helps Agencies Track Waste Online," *Waste & Recycling News*, April 12, 2010.

Nichol Nelson   "Worms Are the Wave of the Future," Slash-food, April 22, 2010. www.slashfood.com.

Sarah Newman   "Artists Saving Our Planet from Plastic," *Huffington Post*, April 21, 2010.

Allison Oswalt   "Step's Junk Funk Finds Beats in Trash," State-Press.com, April 22, 2010. www.statepress.com.

Melissa Rice   "Solving the Problems of Garbage in Space," Space Travel: Exploration and Tourism, November 20, 2008. www.space-travel.com.

Paul H. Rubin   "Environmentalism as Religion," *Wall Street Journal*, April 22, 2010.

Lisa Schlein   "EcoChic Fashion Preserves Biodiversity," Voices of America, January 31, 2010. www.voanews.com.

For Further Discussion

Chapter 1

1. In Diego Cevallos's viewpoint, municipal waste management expert Alfonso De la Torre blames authorities' failure to act on Mexico City's growing garbage problem on "society's resistance to change," political problems, and lack of resources. Do you agree with De la Torre? Why or why not? In your opinion, how could governments encourage greater societal change? How might additional resources help solve problems? According to the other viewpoints in Chapter 1, what factors contribute to the problems of trash?

Chapter 2

1. Kevin Libin expresses that too much recycling actually harms the environment. Why, according to Libin, should there be limits on recycling? What does he think about incineration? What arguments concerning recycling and/or incineration do Leo Hickman and Wang Pan and Li Jianmin offer in their viewpoints? What is your opinion regarding recycling and incineration?

2. Jacob Baynham discusses the environmental catastrophe caused by abandoned vessels. Why, according to Baynham, are these ships so hazardous to the environment and to the health of ship workers? Do you think dismantling old vessels needs to be addressed in a similar way as addressing household waste issues, as described in other viewpoints in the chapter? Why or why not? What are some possible solutions to the problems of both old vessels and household waste?

Chapter 3

1. Katharine Mieszkowsi claims "the lowly plastic bag is an environmental scourge like none other, sapping the life out of our oceans and thwarting our attempts to recycle it." Do you think the small Australian town's methods to get rid of bottled water, as described in the viewpoint by Warren McLaren, could help solve the plastic bag dilemma? It so, which of these methods do you think would work best? Do you have your own ideas on how to solve these problems?

2. Andrew Shakman discusses how food service waste management could benefit both the environment and businesses. Why do you think the food service industry has been so slow to embrace this idea? How might ideas expressed in the other viewpoints in this chapter relate to the waste reduction described by Shakman? Do you think food service businesses could borrow ideas from the other viewpoints? Which ones?

Chapter 4

1. Around the globe, individuals are finding creative ways to deal with the garbage problem. Of the viewpoints, which two do you find the most interesting? Why? What do you think are some limitations of each of the six alternative solutions expressed in Chapter 4? How might these limitations be addressed? If there were no limits on innovation, if anything were possible, what would be your creative solution to our world's garbage dilemma? Describe this solution in one paragraph, and then draw a picture representing the solution.

Organizations to Contact

The editors have compiled the following list of organizations concerned with the issues debated in this book. The descriptions are derived from materials provided by the organizations. All have publications or information available for interested readers. The list was compiled on the date of publication of the present volume; the information provided here may change. Be aware that many organizations take several weeks or longer to respond to inquiries, so allow as much time as possible.

Clean Air Council
135 South Nineteenth Street, Suite 300
Philadelphia, PA   19103
(215) 567-4004 • fax: (215) 567-5791
e-mail: jblack@cleanair.org
Web site: www.cleanair.org

The Clean Air Council is dedicated to protecting everyone's right to breathe clean air. The council works through public education, community advocacy, and government oversight to ensure enforcement of environmental laws. Its Web site provides reports, guides, newsletters, and fact sheets on environmental issues.

Clean Water Action
111 New Montgomery Street #600, San Francisco, CA   94105
(415) 369-9160 • fax: (415) 369-9180
e-mail: cocwa@cleanwater.org
Web site: www.cleanwateraction.org

Clean Water Action works to empower people to take action to protect America's waters, build healthy communities, and to make democracy work for everyone. Clean Water Action uses grassroots organizing, policy research, and political advocacy to pursue environmental protections. Clean Water Action publishes *Currents/Online* as well as reports, fact sheets, and other resources on its Web site.

Collaborative Partnership on Forests (CPF)
UNFF Secretariat, One UN Plaza, DC1-1245
New York, NY 10017
(212) 963-3401 • fax: (917) 367-3186
e-mail: unff@un.org
Web site: www.fao.org/forestry/cpf/en

The Collaborative Partnership on Forests (CPF) is a voluntary arrangement among fourteen international organizations and secretariats with substantial programs on forestry. The CPF supports the United Nations Forum on Forests; promotes the management, conservation, and sustainable development of all types of forests; and strengthens long-term political commitment to this end. The CPF Web site publishes policy documents, progress reports, and other materials relating to forests.

Earth Resource Foundation (ERF)
PO Box 12364, Costa Mesa, CA 92627
(949) 645-5163
e-mail: info@earthresource.org
Web site: www.earthresource.org

Earth Resource Foundation (ERF) is an environmental nonprofit organization developed to empower the general public with the resources needed to make environmentally sustainable choices and changes. ERF's mission is to preserve, conserve, and restore the earth to a healthy and sustainable state by redirecting available human, technological, monetary, and academic resources. The *Circle*, the Earth Resource Foundation newsletter, can be found on the organization's Web site along with other ERF publications and information about pertinent programs and events.

Earth System Governance
International Project Office, IHDP Secretariat (UNU-IHDP),
United Nations Campus, Hermann-Ehlers-Strasse 10
Bonn D-53113
    Germany
+49 (0) 228 815 0635 • fax: +49 (0) 228 815 0620

e-mail: ipo@earthsystemgovernance.org
Web site: www.earthsystemgovernance.org

Earth System Governance advances a scientific plan that changes traditional systems of governance. This plan is organized around five principles: architecture, agency, adaptiveness, accountability, and allocation and access. *Global Climate Governance Beyond 2012: Architecture, Agency and Adaptation* was published by Cambridge University Press in 2010. This and other publications related to Earth System Governance principles can be found on the organization's Web site.

European Environment Agency (EEA)
Kongens Nytorv 6, Copenhagen K   DK-1050
   Denmark
+ 45 33 36 71 00
Web site: www.eea.europa.eu

An agency of the European Union, European Environment Agency's (EEA's) task is to provide sound, independent information on the environment. The EEA is a major information source for the public as well as for those involved in developing, adopting, implementing, and evaluating environment policy. EEA's periodical, *EEA Signals*, as well as other information, is available on the agency's Web site.

Greenpeace International
Ottho Heldringstraat 5, Amsterdam   1066 AZ
   The Netherlands
+31 (0) 20 718 2000 • fax: +31 (0) 20 718 2002
e-mail: supporter.services.int@greenpeace.org
Web site: www.greenpeace.org/international

Greenpeace International is an independent global campaigning organization that acts to change attitudes and behavior, to protect and conserve the environment, and to promote peace. Greenpeace International's efforts involve addressing climate change, protecting oceans and forests, eliminating nuclear weapons and hazardous chemicals, and encouraging sustainable agriculture. Its Web site maintains up-to-date articles, videos, audio recordings, and photos, as well as a climate blog.

Intergovernmental Panel on Climate Change (IPCC)

c/o World Meteorological Organization
7bis Avenue de la Paix, C.P. 2300, Geneva 2   CH-1211
   Switzerland
+41-22-730-8208/54/84 • fax: +41-22-730-8205/13
e-mail: IPCC-Sec@wmo.int
Web site: www.ipcc.ch

Established by the Nations Environment Programme (UNEP) and the World Meteorological Organization (WMO), the Intergovernmental Panel on Climate Change (IPCC) provides the world with a clear scientific view on the current state of climate change and its potential environmental and socioeconomic consequences. The IPCC is a scientific body that reviews and assesses the most recent scientific, technical, and socioeconomic information worldwide relevant to the understanding of climate change. The IPCC's "Assessment Reports" and other materials are available on its Web site. It also publishes a newsletter, *IPCCNews*.

International Human Dimensions Programme on Global Environmental Change (IHDP)

IHDP Secretariat, United Nations University, UN Campus
Hermann-Ehlers-Strasse 10, Bonn   D-53113
   Germany
+49 (0) 228 815 0600 • fax: +49 (0) 228 815 0620
e-mail: secretariat@ihdp.unu.edu
Web site: www.ihdp.unu.edu

The International Human Dimensions Programme on Global Environmental Change (IHDP) works toward understanding and addressing the effects of individuals and societies on global environmental change, and how such global changes, in turn, affect humans. IHDP focuses its activities on three principal areas: developing and sustaining cutting-edge research; developing worldwide capacity to understand and deal with these challenges; and promoting interaction between scientists and policy makers on these topics. IHDP publishes annual reports; committee bulletins; and its periodical, *UGEC Viewpoints*, on its Web site.

Plastic Pollution Coalition
2150 Allston Way, Suite 460, Berkeley, California   94704
(510) 394-5772
e-mail: info@plasticpollutioncoalition.org
Web site: http://plasticpollutioncoalition.org

The mission of the Plastic Pollution Coalition is to stop plastic pollution and its toxic impacts on humans, the environment, and wildlife worldwide. Plastic Pollution Coalition's goals are to build awareness, build a global community, empower action, support legislation, educate, and support scientific advancement. Plastic Pollution Coalition's Web site offers articles and videos about plastic pollution and a calendar of events.

Sierra Club
85 Second Street, 2nd Floor, San Francisco, CA   94105
(415) 977-5500 • fax: (415) 977-5799
e-mail: information@sierraclub.org
Web site: www.sierraclub.org

The Sierra Club works to protect communities, wild places, and the planet itself. Goals of the Sierra Club include moving beyond coal; reducing greenhouse gas emissions; promoting green energy solutions and green transportation; and protecting habitats and communities. Sierra Club publishes *Sierra* magazine, produces videos, and hosts a weekly radio program through Sierra Club Radio.

Story of Stuff Project
1442 A Walnut Street, #272, Berkeley, CA   94709
(510) 883-1055 • fax: (510) 883-1054
e-mail: info@storyofstuff.org
Web site: www.storyofstuff.com

The mission of the Story of Stuff Project is to build a strong, diverse, decentralized, cross-sector movement to transform systems of production and consumption to serve ecological sustainability and social well-being. The Story of Stuff uses public discourse on a diverse set of sustainability issues to build a sustainable and just world. The Story of Stuff Project's Web site includes videos, a blog, and resources concerning sustainability and the environment.

United Nations Environment Programme (UNEP)
United Nations Avenue, Gigiri, PO Box 30552
Nairobi   00100
  Kenya
(254-20) 7621234 • fax: (254-20) 7624489/90
e-mail: unepinfo@unep.org
Web site: www.unep.org

The United Nations Environment Programme (UNEP) has a mission to provide leadership and encourage partnership in caring for the environment by inspiring, informing, and enabling nations and peoples to improve their quality of life without compromising that of future generations. UNEP advocates for environmental responsibility involving all aspects of the earth. In 2010, UNEP published *Clearing the Waters: A Focus on Water Quality Solutions.* Information about this and other UNEP publications, including its periodical, *Our Planet,* can be located on the organization's Web site.

Bibliography of Books

Frank Ackerman — *Why Do We Recycle? Markets, Values, and Public Policy.* Washington DC: Island Press, 1997.

Lori Baird — *Don't Throw It Out: Recycle, Renew and Reuse to Make Things Last.* New York: Rodale, 2007.

Ed Brody, Jay Goldspinner, Katie Green, and Rona Leventhal, eds. — *Spinning Tales, Weaving Hope: Stories, Storytelling and Activities for Peace, Justice and the Environment.* Philadelphia, PA: New Society Publishers, 1992.

Loree Griffin Burns — *Tracking Trash: Flotsam, Jetsam, and the Science of Ocean Motion.* Boston: Houghton Mifflin, 2007.

Daniel C. Esty and Andrew S. Winston — *Green to Gold: How Smart Companies Use Environmental Strategy to Innovate, Create Value, and Build Competitive Advantage.* Hoboken, NJ: Wiley, 2009.

Gil Friend — *The Truth About Green Business.* Upper Saddle River, NJ: FT Press, 2009.

Rosie Harlow and Sally Morgan — *Garbage and Recycling.* New York: Kingfisher, 1995.

Sidney Harris — *There Goes the Neighborhood: Cartoons on the Environment.* Athens: University of Georgia Press, 1996.

Paul Hawken   *Blessed Unrest: How the Largest Move-*
ment in the World Came into Being,
and Why No One Saw It Coming.
New York: Viking, 2007.

Bonnie   *Strand: An Odyssey of Pacific Ocean*
Henderson   *Debris.* Corvallis, OR: Oregon State
University Press, 2008.

Daniel Imhoff *Paper or Plastic: Searching for Solu-*
tions to an Overpackaged World. San
Francisco: Sierra Club Books, 2005.

Barbara   *Animal, Vegetable, Miracle: A Year of*
Kingsolver   *Food Life.* New York: HarperCollins,
2007.

Chris Laszlo   *Sustainable Value: How the World's*
Leading Companies Are Doing Well by
Doing Good. Stanford, CA: Stanford
Business Books, 2008.

Joel Makower *Strategies for the Green Economy: Op-*
portunities and Challenges in the New
World of Business. New York:
McGraw-Hill, 2009.

William   *Cradle to Cradle: Remaking the Way*
McDonough *We Make Things.* New York: North
and Michael   Point Press, 2002.
Braungart

Skye Moody   *Washed Up: The Curious Journeys of*
Flotsam and Jetsam. New York: MJF
Books, 2009.

William Rathje *Rubbish! The Archaeology of Garbage.*
and Cullen   Tucson, AZ: University of Arizona
Murphy   Press, 2001.

Erik Reece   *Lost Mountain: A Year in the Vanishing Wilderness: Radical Strip Mining and the Devastation of Appalachia.* New York: Riverhead Books, 2006.

Heather Rogers   *Gone Tomorrow: The Hidden Life of Garbage.* New York: New Press, 2005.

Harriet Rohmer   *Heroes of the Environment: True Stories of People Who Are Helping to Protect Our Planet.* San Francisco, CA: Chronicle Books, 2009.

Elizabeth Royte   *Bottlemania: How Water Went on Sale and Why We Bought It.* New York: Bloomsbury, 2008.

Elizabeth Royte   *Garbage Land: On the Secret Trail of Trash.* New York: Little, Brown and Company, 2005.

Carl Safina   *Voyage of the Turtle: In Pursuit of the Earth's Last Dinosaur.* New York: Holt, 2006.

Susan Strasser   *Waste and Want: A Social History of Trash.* New York: Metropolitan Books, 1999.

Hans Tammemagi   *The Waste Crisis: Landfills, Incinerators, and the Search for a Sustainable Future.* New York: Oxford University Press, 1999.

Index

Geographic headings and page numbers in **boldface** refer to viewpoints about that country or region.

Numerals

1st Lt. Alex Bonnyman (ship), 119–120, 121, 124

A

Acidification, oceans, 33

Adventure Geology, 31

Agricultural waste pollution, 47, 49

Aid and grants. *See* International grants, environmental projects

Air pollution. *See* Dioxins; Greenhouse gases; Incineration

Albatrosses, 25, 28, 166

Alcohol, as vehicle fuel, 194, 195–198

Alexander, Judd H., 165

Algalita Marine Research Foundation, 23, 131, 136

Allen, Chris, 83–84

Aluminum cans, 164

Aluminum recycling, 82, 96, 100

American Industrial Services, 41

Amsterdam, The Netherlands, *60*

Anaerobic digestion, 111, 152, 192, 196–197, 200

Ancient civilization, 165

Anders (ship), 118–119, 121, 124

Andrews, Paul, 89, 90–91

Animal wastes, 194, 196

Architecture, 170–176

Art, 184–188

A.S.A Internacional (waste management company), 58–59

Asbestos, 121, 122

Attero Recycling, 37

Australia, 138–143

bottled water ban, Bundanoon, 138–143

greenhouse gas emissions, 158

Austria, *60*, 81

B

Baekeland, Leo, 26

Bakelite, 26

Bangladesh, 66–69

Dhaka, waste, 66–69

education opportunities, 66, 68

plastic bag ban, 132

ship steel recycling, 118–125

Basel Action Network (BAN), 37, 120, 122, 124

Basel Convention on the Control of Transboundary Movements of Hazardous Wastes and Their Disposal, 37

Baynham, Jacob, 118–125

Beaches, pollution, 16, 23, 24, 162

See also Oceans

Beasley, Dolores, 202

Belgrade, Serbia, 51, 52, 55–56

Bilge and ballast water, 123

Bio-fermentation, 111

Biodegradability (non-biodegradability)
plastics, 23, 27–28, 128, 130, 132, 135
styrofoam, 15
Biofuels, 190, 191–193, 194–198
Bjarovic, Amela, 51–65
Blazic, Branislav, 58
Bluck, John, 202
Blume, David, 197
Bonny (ship), 119–120, 121, 124
Bordo Poniente dump (Mexico), 70, 71–75
Bottled water
environmental harms, 141–142
history and consumption, 27, 141
town-wide bans, 138–143
See also Plastic bottles
Bottled Water Alliance, 140
BPA (toxin), 17
Brazil, greenhouse gas emissions, 158
Brominated flame retardants, 44
Brundtland Commission (United Nations), 155
Bundanoon, Australia, 138–143
Bureaucracy, recycling in construction, 170, 173–175
Burning. See Incineration
Burtinshaw, Julie, 135
Butalia, Urvashi, 101–106

C

Cadmium, 44
Calgary, Alberta, Canada, 93–96
California, plastic bag policy, 16, 98, 131, 133–134, 136
Canada, 93–100, 160–167
Calgary curbside recycling, and concerns, 93–100
greenhouse gas emissions, 158
Montreal arts, 185–186
packaging waste awareness, 160–167
Cardboard
packaging, 161
recycling, 83
CEEF (closed ecology experiment facility), 203
Cell phones. See E-waste
Cevallos, Diego, 70–75
Child health
Bangladesh waste-pickers, 66, 67–68
e-waste toxins, 41–42
water pollution and diarrheal diseases, 48
China, 107–113, 114–117, 184–188
e-waste, 36, 42, 43
economic evolution, 87, 117
everyday environmental mind-sets, 114–117
greenhouse gas emissions, 158
incinerator protest, 107–113
per-person waste statistics, 108, 109, 110
recycling buyer, UK materials, 79–80, 81, 82, 83–84
trash into art, 184–188
Western businesses' disposable culture, 114, 115–116, 117
CO_2 emissions
countries, rankings, 158
European cities, rankings, 60
Co-mingled recycling collection, 82, 84, 85, 100, 159
Coal-fired power plants, 90, 99
Coca-Cola, 166

Commercial composting
    collection from households, 102, 132–133
    facilities, 151

Community action
    bottled water bans, 138–143
    e-waste prevention, 43
    incinerator protests, 107, 108, 110

Compostable disposables, 147, 150

Composting
    city recycling services, 102, 132–133
    food waste management, 146, 147, 148, 149, 150–151, 152
    homes, 159
    paper bags, 131, 136

Computers. *See* E-waste

Confiscated alcohol, 195–196

Consumerism
    e-waste growth, 14, 40–41
    major waste contribution, 86–87, 114, 115–116, 163
    U.S. history, 14
    See also "Reduce, reuse, recycle"

Copenhagen, Denmark
    conference on global warming, 2009, 52
    as green city, *60*

Corporate social responsibility
    extended producer responsibility, 165–166
    hypocrisy, waste creation, 115

Curbside (sorted) recycling
    Calgary program and concerns, 93–96, 98
    vs. co-mingled, 82, 84, 85, 88, 100, 159
    vs. drop-off/consumer-initiated, 94, 97, 101–102
    plastic bags, 133
    program introductions, 162
    Yokohama, Japan, rules, 101–103

D

Dataquest, 35–38

DDT (toxin), 25, 26

De la Torre, Alfonso, 71–72, 72–73, 75

Deep space exploration, 199, 200–203

Dehydration of waste, 152

Delgado, Martha, 74

Denmark
    Copenhagen as green city, *60*
    Copenhagen conference, 2009, 52
    incineration, 99

Dhaka, Bangladesh, 66–69

Dhaka Courier, 66–69

Diarrheal diseases, 48

Dioxins, 90, 108

"Disposable culture," 14, 87, 114, 115–116, 130, 163

Downcycling, 134–135

Doy pack recycling, 180–183

Dr. Seuss, 15

Drago, Tito, 154–159

Dulic, Oliver, 54, 57, 65

Dumps. *See* Landfills

E

E-waste
    Africa, dumping, 41, 80
    Asia, dumping, 41
    China, 36
    Europe and Japan, 38
    India, 35–38
    Latin America, dumping, 41

re-use, 116
United States, 14, 39–44
Earth Day, 15
Eco-art, 184–188
Ecosystems, pollution effects, 23, 25, 33, 45–50, 120–121
Educational system, Bangladesh, 66, 68
Egypt, 45–50
Electronics manufacturers, responsibilities, 42–43, 43–44
See also E-waste
Electronics TakeBack Coalition, 40, 42–43, 44
Electronics waste. *See* E-waste
Energy generation
food/organic waste sources, 151, 153, 156, 190–193
incineration, 88, 89–90, 99
waste and recycling potential, 57, 59, 73, 99
England. *See* United Kingdom
Environmental justice issues
exporting e-waste, 35, 36, 37–38, 39, 40, 41–42
hazardous work conditions, recycling, 118, 120–121
waste picking and caste, 66, 67–69, 105
Environmental Protection Agency (EPA)
e-waste information, 41, 44
food waste calculator, 150
reduce, reuse, recycle information, 97
ships, toxins regulations, 121, 124
Enviropower (energy firm), 89–91
Ethanol. *See* Biofuels
Europe
e-waste, 38
greenest cities, *60*

European Bank for Reconstruction and Development (EBRD), 63
European Green City Index, 60
European Space Agency (ESA), 200
Excell, Jon, 199–203
Exporting and importing of waste
e-waste, 35, 36, 37–38, 39, 40, 41–42
landfill waste, 163
Extended producer responsibility, 165–166

F

Fashion statements, 137
Fast food chains, 114, 115–116, 117, 162
Fish stocks
Nile River, 45–46, 49–50
oceans, 33
Fishes. *See* Fish stocks; Marine life
Flexible fuel vehicles, 192
Food donation, 147, 149
Food service waste management
best practices, 146–148
China, Western chains' waste, 114, 115–116, 117
United States, 144–153
waste management hierarchy, 147
Food waste
Bangladesh, 67
reduction, waste management, 144–153, 192
tracking, 149–150
United Kingdom, waste collection, 86
Fortson, Danny, 189–193
France, greenhouse gas emissions, 158
Free trade agreements, 38
Freyberg, Tom, 84

Frugality and thrift
  environmental benefits, 87
  Great Depression and culture,
  14–15
Fund for Environmental Protection, 57, 64
Fung, Micky, 184, 188

G

Garbage boats, 100
Garbage collection. *See* Recycling;
  Trucks, garbage and recycling;
  Waste management
Garbage disposals, 151–152
Garbage Warrior (documentary),
  173
Geisel, Theodor, 15
Geothermal energy usage, 172,
  175
Germany
  greenhouse gas emissions, 158
  plastic recycling, 96–97
  refillable bottles policy, 164
Glass recycling, 82, 95–96, 156,
  159
Global Alliance for Incinerator
  Alternatives/Global Anti-
  Incinerator Alliance (GAIA), 112
Global financial crisis
  consumerism lead-up/cause,
  14
  positive environmental side
  effects, 16
Global warming, 30, 31, 33, 52
Gmizic, Dragan, 51–65
Godfrey, Mark, 114–117
Gou Fu Mao, 114–117
Gradska Cistoca (waste management company), 55
Grant, Richard, 21–34
Grants. *See* International grants,
  environmental projects

Great Pacific Garbage Patch, 21–
  23, 26, 28–30, 131
Green Seal GS-46 Environmental
  Standard for Restaurants and
  Foodservices, 148
Green technology
  architecture and construction,
  170–176
  e-waste avoidance needs,
  43–44
  job creation potential, 65
  recycling, 82
  waste disposal, 150–152, 199,
  200–203
  waste tracking, 149–150
  See also Anaerobic digestion;
  Biofuels
Greenhouse gases
  bottled water production, 141
  emissions by country, 158
  emitted by dumps and landfills, 52, 70, 71, 89, 111, 153
  emitted by vehicles, 71, 75
  European cities' CO2, 60
  incinerator- vs. coal-generated
  energy, 90, 99
Greenpeace, 122, 159
Greenstar (materials recovery
  firm), 79, 81
groundwater pollution, 72, 73,
  111, 189–190
Group2WP, 48
Guangzhou, China, 107, 108–113

H

Hall, Philip, 189, 190–193
Hazardous work conditions
  fishing, polluted waters, 45,
  47–49
  steel recycling, 118, 120–121,
  122
  waste picking, 66, 67–68, 69

Health and sanitation
  Dhaka, Bangladesh waste, 66–69
  epidemics, poor waste management, 52, 63
  incineration dangers, 112, 159
  Nile River pollution and health, 45, 47–49
  ship scrapping dangers, 118, 120, 122
Heyerdahl, Thor, 31
Hickman, Leo, 78–92
Hindmarch, Anya, 137
Hodge, Oliver, 173
Hosking, Rebecca, 25
Hospital waste, 66, 67, 68
Human wastes, 194, 196, 200, 203
Hume, Christopher, 160–167

I

IKEA, 137
Illegal waste
  dumps and dumping, 72–73
  e-waste trade, 35, 37–38, 41
  legal loopholes and ship scrapping, 118–125
  See also Exporting and importing of waste
Importing and exporting, waste. *See* Exporting and importing of waste
Incineration
  China, plans and protests, 107–113
  choices vs. recycling, 78, 80–81, 98–99, 111
  city incinerators, 81, 89–91
  energy generation method, 88, 89–90, 99
  environmental impact, 88–91, 99, 108, 159
  health dangers, 112, 159
  inevitability, 87–88

India, 35–38, 101–106
  e-waste, 35–38
  garbage and recycling, 101–106, 182
  greenhouse gas emissions, 158
  recycling buyer, UK materials, 81
  ship steel recycling, 118–125
  waste generation, 105
Indonesia, greenhouse gas emissions, 158
Industrial pollutants, 47, 48
Industrialization, 15
Infectious disease risks
  poor waste management, 52, 63
  toilet and hospital waste, 66, 68
Institute of Mechanical Engineers, 88
International grants, environmental projects
  art prizes, 185–188
  Serbian waste management, 56, 57, 63, 64
  SMART competition, 31
International Space Station, 202–203
Ireland, plastic bag tax, 16, 131–132
Italy, greenhouse gas emissions, 158
Ithula, Maore, 112

J

Japan, 101–106
  e-waste, 38
  economic history, 87
  environmental policy history, 104
  garbage and recycling, 101–106

greenhouse gas emissions, 158
incineration, 99
Jozefowicz, Chris, 39–44

K

Kennedy, Jane, 84–85
KFC, 115, 116, 117
Khullar, Mridu, 182
KILUS Foundation, 180–183
Kitchen waste, 146, 147, 149
Kyle, Barbara, 40, 42–43, 44

L

Lake Merritt Institute, 129
Landfills
    Bangladesh, 67
    Canada, 161, 162–163, 164
    China, 107, 110, 111
    England, 80, 81, 85, 91, 190,
        191
    environmental impact, and
        alternatives, 80, 81, 88–90,
        91, 111
    fees, 81, 91, 98, 190
    food service waste avoidance,
        148–149, 153
    greenhouse gas creation, 52,
        70, 71, 89, 111, 153, 189–190
    North America, 98, 99–100
    Serbia, 51, 52–65
Lasseur, Christophe, 200, 201,
    202–203
Lead and lead poisoning, 42, 44,
    121, 122
Legislation, environmental
    Japan, 104
    needs, 16, 113
Lemna International, 59
Li Jianmin, 107–113
Libin, Kevin, 93–100
The Lorax (Dr. Seuss), 15

M

Madrid, Spain, 154, 155, 157
Marine ecosystems, 23, 25, 33,
    45–50, 120–121
Marine life
    fish stocks, 33, 45–46, 49–50
    plastics' harms, 16, 23, 25–26,
        28, 128, 129–130, 131, 135,
        162, 166–167
Marketing and public awareness,
    plastics, 29–31, 32–33, 137
McDonald's, 114, 115, 116, 117
McGrath, Cam, 45–50
McLaren, Warren, 138–143
Medical waste. *See* Hospital waste
MELiSSA system (Micro-
    Ecological Life Support System
    Alternative), 199, 200–203
Mercury, 26, 44, 122
Metal recycling
    post-consumer, 82, 83, 95–96,
        100
    ships, scrap, 118–125
Mexico, 70–75
    greenhouse gas emissions, 158
    waste and space challenges,
        70–75
    Mexico City, 70–75
Midway Island, 25
Mieszkowski, Katharine, 128–137
Mir (space station), 202
Mobile phones. *See* E-waste
Montreal, Canada, 185–186
Moore, Charles, 22–24, 32

N

NASA, 202
National security, 16
Native American values, 15

Navy ships
  as ocean polluters, 23
  recycling, 118–120
Netherlands, *60*
New York City, 98
Niiler, Pearn, 26
Nile River, 45–50
North Pacific Subtropical Gyre, 22, 131
Norway, *60*
Nurdles, 24
Nylon, 27

O

Oceans
  global warning and acidification, 33
  overfishing, 33
  plastic pollution, 21–34, 131, 135, 166–167
Off-grid living, 172, 175
Oil, waste, 123
Oil use. *See* Biofuels; Petroleum inventions and innovations; Petroleum use, plastic
Oslo, Norway, *60*
Outer space recycling, 199–203
Overfishing
  Nile River, 45–46, 50
  oceans, 33

P

Pacific Ocean. *See* Great Pacific Garbage Patch; North Pacific Subtropical Gyre
Packaging
  Canada addresses waste, 160–167
  consumer choices and, 97
  excess, recycling challenges, 87
  food service waste, 114, 115–116, 117, 144, 146–147, 153, 162
  producers reduce waste, 166
  recycling into consumer products, 137, 177, 180–183
  See also Bottled water; "Throwaway culture"
Packard, Vance, 87
Pakistan, steel ship recycling, 118–125
Paper bags, 17, 131, 136–137
Paper recycling and market, 79–80, 82–84, 96, 100, 116–117
Pavlovic, Biljana, 51–65
PCBs (polychlorinated biphenyls), 25, 26, 90, 120–121, 122, 124
Per-person waste statistics
  China, 108, 109, 110
  Serbia, 54
  Spain, 154
  United Kingdom, 189–190
Persistent organic pollutants, 25, 26, 90, 120–121, 122, 124
PET (polyethylene terephthalate), 32, 80
Petroleum inventions and innovations, 26–27
Petroleum use, plastic
  market fluctuations, 117
  plastic bags, 16, 17, 128, 130, 135, 136
  plastic bottles, 97, 141
Pfc. James Anderson Jr. (ship), 118–120, 121, 124
Philippines, 177–183
Photodegradation, plastics, 23–24
Plankton, 23, 25–26, 30, 131
Planned obsolescence, 14, 87
  See also Consumerism
Plant recycling, 177, 178–180

Plastic bags
  alternatives to using, 16–17, 27, 32, 136
  animal deaths, 16, 25, 128, 129–130, 131, 135, 162, 166–167
  bans, 16, 131–132, 136
  costs, and item pricing, 16, 136
  history, 27, 130
  industry, 131
  lifespan/decomposition rates and effects, 128, 130, 132, 135
  recycling difficulty and costs, 98, 128, 130, 132–136
  taxation, 16, 131–132, 137, 167
  usage and disposal rates, 15, 27, 130, 135
Plastic bottles
  alternatives, 17, 32, 138, 140, 162
  recycling and market, 117, 142
  toxins, 17
  usage and disposal, 27, 105, 141–142
Plastics
  industry, 32
  innovation history and types, 26–27
  lifespan/decomposition rates and effects, 15–16, 23–24, 27–28, 128, 130, 132, 135
  ocean pollution, 16, 21–34, 162
  packaging, 161
  recycling, 27, 32, 69, 79, 81–82, 86, 96–98, 117, 128, 130, 132–136, 142
  See also Plastic bags; Plastic bottles
Plastiki (boat), 28–30, 31, 32–33
Plate waste, 146, 147

Poland, greenhouse gas emissions, 158
Pollution control laws, Japan, 104
Polyethylene, 134
  See also PET (polyethylene terephthalate); Plastic bags
Popovic, Sanja, 56, 57
Porter, J. Winston, 95, 100
Post-consumer food waste, 146, 147
Power generation. *See* Energy generation
Pre-consumer food waste, 146, 147, 149
Private sector waste management, 57–59, 62, 74
PRNewswire-Asia, 184–188
Public-governmental communication, 112–113
Public opinion
  incinerator programs, 107–113
  recycling, 80–92, 94
Puod, Ana, 177–183
PVC (polyvinyl chloride), 26–27

R

Read, Adam, 88–89
Recycled items
  art, 184–188
  boats, 28–30, 31, 32–33
  housing, 134, 170–176
  paper bags, 131, 137
  Philippines industries, 177–183
  roads, 182
Recycling
  Calgary, Alberta, 93–96, 98
  co-mingled vs. curbside/sorted, 82, 84, 85, 88, 100, 159
  e-waste, 35, 36, 37, 41, 42–43, 44

excess packaging, 87
facilities described, 79–80
facilities/processes described, 81–83, 133
ideal rates, 93, 95, 100
vs. incineration, 88–89, 91, 98–99, 111
Mexico plans, 72, 73
outer space, 199–203
program funding by industries, 165–166
"reduce, reuse, recycle" hierarchy, 16, 86–87, 97, 163–164
reuse as, 103–104, 105
rules and social pressure, 91–92, 94–95, 101–103
sale markets, 69, 79–80, 82–85, 95–99, 117, 134
Serbia, 51, 53, 56, 57, 59–60, 64–65
Spain, 154, 156, 157, 159
value debated, 78–92, 93–100
See also Recycled items; specific materials
Redford, Robert, 16
"Reduce, reuse, recycle"
hierarchy, 16, 86–87, 97, 163–164
ideas, 16–17
source reduction, food waste management, 147, 148–150
Refillable bottle laws, 164
Renewable energy use
recycled homes, 172, 175
Spain, goals, 156
Repair and repair industries, 87, 97
Reusable items
cups and mugs, 115, 147, 162
shopping bags, 16–17, 114, 116, 133–134, 136, 137
soft drink bottles, 164
trash-picked, 68, 103–104, 105, 116–117

water bottles, 17, 105, 138, 140, 164
Reuse
daily living, 17, 97, 114, 115, 116
India, reuse as recycling, 103–104, 105
Philippines, reuse as recycling, 177–183
plastic bags, rather than recycling, 133–134, 136, 137
plastics, design and purpose, 31–32
"reduce, reuse, recycle" hierarchy, 16, 86–87, 97
repair, 87, 97
See also Reusable items
Reynolds, Michael, 170–176
Roberts, Jennifer, 43
Rothschild, David de, 21, 28–31, 32–34
Royle, Jo, 31
Rules, recycling, 101–103, 134
Russia
greenhouse gas emissions, 158
incineration, 99

S

San Francisco, California
city recycling, 132–133
plastic bag ban, 16, 131, 136
plastic bag recycling, 98, 132–134, 136
Sánchez, Jorge, 72–73
Sanitation. *See* Health and sanitation; Waste management
Saudi Arabia, greenhouse gas emissions, 158
Sea animals. *See* Marine life
Seabirds, 25, 28, 128, 131, 135
See also Marine life

Serbia, 51–65
per-person waste statistics, 54
waste management challenges, 51–65
Seuss, Dr., 15
Sevier, Laura, 170–176
Sewage discharging
food waste, 151–152
Nile River, 47, 49
Shakman, Andrew, 144–153
Ships
garbage barges, 100
ocean garbage dumping, 23
ship scrapping, 118–125
Shopping bags. *See* Paper bags; Plastic bags; Reusable items
Simonovic, Milos, 56
Sludge, 90, 123
SMART competition, 31
Soft drink packaging, 164
Solar energy usage, 172, 175
Source reduction, food waste management, 147, 148–150
South Africa
e-waste, 36
greenhouse gas emissions, 158
South Asia, 118–125
Space constraints, landfills
China, 107
Mexico City, 70–75
Ontario, Canada, 161
perceptions, North America, 99–100
Spain, 154–159
greenhouse gas emissions, 158
improving garbage management, 154–159
per-person waste statistics, 154
Spears, Greg, 41
Sredojevic, Milomir, 62
SS *Oceanic* (ship), 121

St. Kitts and Nevis, 119, 120, 121
Star Maritime Corp., 119–120
Starbucks, 114, 115, 117
Steel recycling
post-consumer waste, 83, 95–96
ships, scrap, 118–125
Stockholm, Sweden, *60*
Styrofoam, 15, 22
Sugiyama, Taisha, 104
Sustainability goals, cities and countries, 154, 155–156, 194
Sustainability ratings systems, 148
Sustainable housing, 170–176
Sustainable Sites Act (2007), 175
Sweden, 194–198
green cars, 198
recycling/incineration opinions, 98–99
Stockholm as green city, *60*
waste into vehicle fuel, 194–198
Sweeney, Doc, 197
Synthetic polymers, 26–27

T

Taiwan, 87
Tap water
bottled, disguised, and sold, 138, 142
production, environmental aspects, 141
Taxes
excessive household waste, 86
garbage production, 167
"green," 154, 155
landfills, 81, 91, 98, 190
plastic bags, 16, 131–132, 137, 167
recycling, 80
TBT (tributyltin), 120–121

Technological innovations. *See* Green technology

Televisions, 41, 42

See also E-waste

Thermal degradation, 111

Thomas, Valerie, 41, 43–44

Thrift. *See* Frugality and thrift

"Throwaway culture," 14, 87, 114, 115–116, 130, 163

Tim Hortons, 162

Tires

manufacturing responsibilities, 164

material, recycled homes, 170–171, 172

Touchmedia Eco-Art China Competition, 184, 185–188

Toxic Free UC, 43

Toxic Substances Control Act (1976), 121

Toxins

air pollution, 90, 108

bioaccumulation, 25–26

bottled water findings, 17, 142

e-waste, 37, 39, 40, 41–42, 43, 44

industrial and agricultural wastes, water, 47, 48, 49

persistent organic pollutants, 25, 26, 90, 120–121, 122, 124

plastics, attraction, 25

plastics, emissions and leaching, 15–16, 17

toxic waste, incineration dangers, 112, 159

toxic waste, steel ship recycling, 118, 120–121, 122–123, 124–125

Tracking systems, waste, 144, 149–150

Trade of waste. *See* Exporting and importing of waste; Illegal waste

Trash-picking. *See* Waste pickers

Trees, 136

Trex, 134

Trivan, Goran, 55

Trucks, garbage and recycling

alternatives to vehicle-transported waste, 100, 157

city needs, 72, 75

green transportation improvements, 156, 196

as polluters, 75, 98

Turkey, greenhouse gas emissions, 158

Turtles, 16, 25, 128, 129, 131, 162, 166

See also Marine life

Typhoon Ketsana (2009), 179, 180

U

Ukraine, greenhouse gas emissions, 158

Underground waste collection, 157

United Kingdom, 78–92, 189–193

greenhouse gas emissions, 158

incineration, 78, 80–81, 89–91, 99

per-person waste statistics, 189–190

plastic bags, history and usage, 27

value of recycling debated, 78–92

waste into fuel entrepreneurship, 189–193

United Nations Environment Programme

budget, 34

reports, plastics, 23, 25, 131

United States, 39–44, 128–137, 144–153, 170–176

e-waste responsibilities, 39–44

food service waste management, 144–153

greenhouse gas emissions, 158

Navy ships, scrap recycling, 118–120
plastic bags, 128–137
recycled home construction, 170–176
waste generation, 100
U.S. Maritime Administration (MARAD), 121

V

Vehicles
air pollution, 71, 75, 90
alternatives to vehicle-transported waste, 157
biofuel production, 189, 190, 191–193, 194–198
ethanol-run, benefits, 198
flexible fuel, 192
garbage and recycling trucks, 72, 75, 98, 100, 156, 196
Vienna, Austria, *60, 81*
Virilio, Paul, 26
Voluntary programs
Canadian waste management, 164
Serbian waste management regulations, 54

W

Wakabayashi, Masayo, 104
Wakelin, Ian, 81–82
Wal-Mart, 166
Wang Pan, 107–113
Ward, Phillip, 85–86, 87–88
Waste and Resources Action Programme (UK), 85
Waste dehydration, 152
Waste generation statistics
China, 108–109, 110
Dhaka, Bangladesh, 66–67
India, increases, 105
Mexico, 70–71, 74

Ontario, Canada, 163
Serbia, 54
Spain, 154
United Kingdom, 189–190, 191
United States, 40, 100, 135
The Waste Makers (Packard), 87
Waste management
Bangladesh, 66–69
best practices, 146–148
environmental impacts, study, 88–89
hierarchy, 147
Mexico, space issues, 70–75
Serbia, 51–65
space exploration, 199, 200–203
Spain, improvements, 154–159
underground systems, 157
United States, food service, 144–153
See also Recycling; Waste reduction
Waste pickers
Bangladesh, and social strata, 66, 67–69
India, 105
professional recyclers, China, 114, 116–117
Waste reduction
area initiatives, 156–157, 159
source reduction, food waste management, 147, 148–150
Waste tracking systems, 144, 149–150
Wastewater
discharging, 47
treatment, 151–152
Water bottles. *See* Plastic bottles
Water lilies, 177, 178–180
Water pollution
Africa-wide, 48
Nile River, 45–50

plastics, 15–16, 21–34, 128, 129–131, 135, 162, 166–167

seaside steel recycling, 118, 120–125

waste runoff, percolation, and seepage, 72, 73, 111, 189–190

Water reuse and recycling, 156, 202–203

Water security, 48

Welsh, Moira, 160–167

Western businesses, 114, 115–116, 117

Whales, 25–26

See also Marine life

Wiles, David, 194–198

World Commission on the Environment and Development (United Nations), 155

Y

Yard waste, 98

Yokohama, Japan, 102–103

Youth, environmental campaigns, 43

Z

Zapatero, José Luis Rodríguez, 155, 156

Zdravkovic, Dragan, 59

"Zero waste" goals, 148–149, 164–165